Quilting Teachers Welcome the New *Quilts! Quilts!! Quilts!!!*

Quilts! Quilts!! Quilts!!! is by far the best book for quilters of any skill level. It is the key that unlocks the door to a long and happy journey down the path of quiltmaking. When I owned a shop, I recommended and sold this book more than any other. Now, as a teacher, I encourage my students to treat themselves to *Quilts! Quilts!! Quilts!!!* for a lifetime of motivation, ideas, and guidance.

> —*Kathleen C. Pappas, quilting teacher, Los Angeles, CA*

If you can afford only one quilting book in a lifetime, buy the one that gives you the most—*Quilts! Quilts!! Quilts!!!* This book carries the novice through the maze of tools to buy, color selection, and piecing, seaming, and assembly techniques. It starts you out with simple, yet elegant patterns. Anyone can make a quilt from this book!

> —*Barbara J. Wilson, quilting teacher, Citrus Heights, CA*

Quilts! Quilts!! Quilts!!! helped put my quilt shop on the map. It has been one of my favorite books from the first day I picked it up. It gives new quilters a good solid understanding of quilting and teaches them to love it. It is a joy to see the smiles of pride and new confidence as that first quilt top comes together.

> —*Gloria M. Park, quilting teacher and former owner of Country Dry Goods, Vancouver, WA*

Quilts! Quilts!! Quilts!!! is an indispensable book for quilters of all levels. I use it for beginning quilt classes in my shop. I especially appreciate the accurate fabric requirements for different sizes of quilts.

> —*Louise Horkey, quilting teacher and partner/owner of Whiffle Tree Quilts, Cupertino, CA*

I have a lot of students who are just beginning their adventure in quilting and they learn the very best techniques using this book. This class fills every time!

> —*LaVonne J. Horner, quilting teacher, Fabric Works, Superior, WI*

Quilts! Quilts!! Quilts!!! has been a hit at my shop since day one with all levels of quilters. I've taught sixteen sampler classes from it, so there are hundreds of quilts out there from my area alone. I love the charts with the fabric requirements for all sizes as well as the clear-cut instructions.

> —*Jean Wells, owner, The Stitchin' Post, Sisters, OR*

Quilts! Quilts!! Quilts!!! has been a consistent best seller in my quilt shop since it was first introduced. We have used the book in classes and recommend it to anyone who wishes to get started making a quilt. The excellent instructions give both the beginner and the more experienced quilter the ability to try any of the projects with great success. The book is also a wonderful reference for any questions a quilter may encounter. The updates and additions in this new edition make *Quilts! Quilts!! Quilts!!!* an outstanding teaching tool.

> —*Jean Humenansky, owner, The Country Peddler Quilt Shop, St. Paul, MN*

QUILTS! QUILTS!! QUILTS!!!

The Complete Guide to Quiltmaking

SECOND EDITION

DIANA McCLUN AND
LAURA NOWNES

PHOTOGRAPHY BY SHARON RISEDORPH

The Quilt Digest Press

Library of Congress Cataloging-in-Publication Data

McClun, Diana
    Quilts! quilts!! quilts!!! : the complete guide to quiltmaking /
    Diana McClun and Laura Nownes. –2nd ed.
        p. cm.
        Includes index.
    ISBN 0-8442-2617-3
    1. Patchwork—Patterns. 2. Quilting—Patterns. 3. Machine quilting—Patterns.
    I. Nownes, Laura.   II. Title
    TT835.M39935   1997
    746.46'041—dc21   97-2537
                                      CIP

Editorial and production direction by Anne Knudsen.

Book design by Kajun Graphics, San Francisco.

Editing by Karen Steib.

Technical editing by Kandy Petersen and Janet Wickell.

Technical drawings by Kandy Petersen.

Cover design by Kim Bartko.

Cover photograph © 1997 by Chris Cassidy, Chicago.

Published by The Quilt Digest Press
An imprint of NTC/Contemporary Publishing Company
4255 West Touhy Avenue
Lincolnwood (Chicago), Illinois 60646-1975, U.S.A.
Copyright © 1997, 1988 by Diana McClun and Laura Nownes.
All rights reserved. No part of this book may be reproduced, stored in a retrieval
system, or transmitted in any form or by any means, electronic, mechanical,
photocopying, recording or otherwise, without the prior permission of
NTC/ Contemporary Publishing Company.
Printed in Hong Kong by Wing King Tong Co. Ltd.
International Standard Book Number: 0-8442-2617-3

Title page photograph:
The power of simplicity is underscored in Bear's Paw (see page 53), made by River City Quilters Guild. The wall quilt, Sawtooth Star (see page 40), was made by Katie Prindle. Both quilts are constructed in a diagonal set with an alternate block. Photographed at the home of Tricia and Steve Thomas.

PREFACE

 Over the years, we have loved hearing the comments you, our readers, have sent about *Quilts! Quilts!! Quilts!!!* Many of you selected it as a guide when making your first quilts, while others use it as a text and reference for quilting classes. We are delighted that some of you even call our book your "Quilting Bible." We were overjoyed when we heard the story of a child who had taken *Quilts! Quilts!! Quilts!!!* from the family bookshelf, read it, and constructed a quilt of her own. These gratifying, personal stories warm our hearts with great appreciation.

Thank you for according us these honors that have encouraged us to update the book into a second edition. We hope, as your words have done for us, that our book encourages you to renew your love for quilts. It is our wish you will surround yourself with mesmerizing, colorful fabric that sings to you as you select your next quilt pattern.

Dear readers, we share with you our experience and expertise to help you enjoy this most rewarding and creative of experiences. From planning to completion, every aspect of quiltmaking is exciting. Continue to create lovingly and joyfully, allow the warm familiarity of your quilts to fill your homes and those of the people you love.

Diana & Laura

Relax for a day in this beautiful garden with Double Nine-Patch Variation, see page 26,
made by Diana McClun and Laura Nownes and machine quilted by Kathy Sandbach.
Photographed at the home of Freddy and Neil Moran.

The scrap Pineapple Log Cabin, see page 68, made by Freddy Moran, is the perfect bed quilt with its multi-colored border that frames the edge of the bed. The vibrantly colored walls contrast with the pristine starched white linens to compliment the quilt. Photographed at the home of Freddy and Neil Moran.

The wall quilt is Pine Tree, see page 50, made by Laura's friendship group, Lavender Bags. The bed quilt, Pineapple Log Cabin, see page 68, was made by Dorie Whipple. The home of Margaret and Volney Peters is filled with items from the nation's past and they give these new but traditional quilts a feeling of belonging. Photographed at the home of Margaret and Volney Peters.

The Log Cabin quilt, see page 18, made by Diana McClun and Laura Nownes,
set against the piles of wood on the veranda gives a sense of history in a rustic setting. The Log Cabin
is a tribute to the past. Photographed at the home of Tricia and Steve Thomas.

The collection of bears gives the Gingerbread House quilt, see page 64, a whimsical setting.
This original design was created by Diana McClun and Laura Nownes and machine quilted by
Kathy Sandbach. Photographed at the home of Margaret and Volney Peters.

In this family room, the Madison House quilt, see page 46, sets the tone from dawn to dusk, as the family enjoys naming the birds found in the fabrics of the quilt. Photographed at the home of Tricia and Steve Thomas.

Fruits and vegetables are the inspiration for the collection of fabrics used to make this Pinwheel quilt,
see page 32, made by Diana McClun and Laura Nownes and machine quilted by Kathy Sandbach.
The early morning sun gives vibrancy to the saturated colors of the Moran home.
Photographed at the home of Freddy and Neil Moran.

Flowers bring both beauty and inspiration when it comes to quiltmaking. This dining room has the perfect painted brick wall for LaVonne J. Horner's sampler quilt, see page 144, surrounded by tulips, sweet peas, and lilac bouquets. Photographed at the home of Tricia and Steve Thomas.

*With a delightful mix of old and new, the Early American setting showcases this
traditionally colored sampler quilt, see page 145, made by Patti Scott-Baier and hand quilted
by Mary Bertken. Photographed at the home of Margaret and Volney Peters.*

The outdoor setting takes us back to a nineteenth-century wash day. Rolled into the antique washing machine is Hopscotch Nine-Patch, see page 29. The quilts on the clothesline are Lawry's sampler on the left, see page 144, Blossoming Tree in the middle, see page 72, and Thousand Pyramids on the right, see page 58. Photographed at the home of Tricia and Steve Thomas.

All Stars, see page 82, made by Dafri Estes and machine quilted by Kathy Sandbach is the perfect companion for the weathered wooden garden chair. Photographed at the home of Freddy and Neil Moran.

Acknowledgments

With grateful hearts we wish to thank all those who helped make our second edition a reality.

Thanks, a big, big thanks to:

Anne Knudsen, our editor, for her ideas, skills, and advice in putting this book together.

Kim Bartko our art director who traveled to California to lend us her expertise.

Sharon Risedorph our photographer for her outstanding work and for her kind and generous nature that made the work enjoyable and fun.

Kandy Petersen whose computer graphic skills brought us beautiful illustrations.

Pat Koren and Laurie Smith of Kajun Graphics for the book design.

Harold Nadel who edited our first edition with nurturing and supportive guidance.

Sue Bowen who shared her teaching skills.

Katie Prindle, Gayle Wells, and Sandy Klop for their sewing help in construction and bindings.

Rosalee Sanders, Dena Canty, Alex Anderson, Dorie Whipple, Gai Perry, Pat Callis, Dafri Estes, Kandy Petersen, Freddy Moran, Barbara Wilson, LaVonne J. Horner, Cynthia Sherburne, Patti Scott-Baier, and Lawry Thorn for composing quilts that brought us a wide range of styles.

Kathy Sandbach, Barbara Wilson, Dorie Whipple, Debra Dann, Paula Reid, Katrina Beverage, and Angelia Haworth for their creative machine stitches that gave the quilts their spirit.

Anna Venti, Mary Bertken, Kristina Volker, and Mirian Patsworth for their nimble fingers that produced such fine hand quilting.

Barbara Engelking, LaVonne J. Horner, Dale Fleming, and Angie Dawson Woolman for their creative use of color and their willingness to experiment with only a line drawing for inspiration.

Freddy and Neil Moran, Margaret and Volney Peters, and Tricia and Steve Thomas for graciously lending their homes for the environment photography.

Adrian Gallardo, Renee Isabelle Walker of Stephen/Reed Flowers, Lafayette, California, for their enthusiasm and expertise as stylists.

Most of all we are indebted to our husbands, David and Bill, who gave their help, support, and love.

TABLE OF CONTENTS

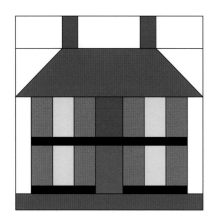

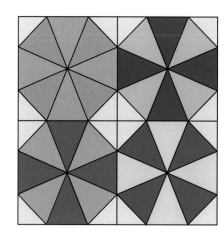

1	Pieced block	7	Post	13	Straight border
2	Appliquéd block	8	Straight set	14	Mitered border
3	Alternate block	9	Diagonal set	15	Quilting design
4	Corner triangle	10	Inner border	16	Batting
5	Side triangle	11	Outer border	17	Backing
6	Sashing	12	Corner block	18	Binding

Introduction

THE ESSENTIALS

 A quilt is more than fabric, batting and stitches. It is a rare and wonderful creation of the soul which expresses our personal statements, our likes and dislikes, feelings, thoughts and loves. It is a bridge that encourages friendships. It supports our need for recognition, as we display it proudly to the applause of its admirers. And it links us with those who've stitched before and those who w'll follow, as it gives a wordless but meaningful description of who we are and what we feel. A quilt is all these—and more: it is the embodiment of love.

Quilts give us a chance to express our need for giving. A dear member of the group was moving away, so Laura's quilting circle decided to express their love and treasured friendship. They constructed a quilt in her favorite colors, peach and green. Each quilter chose her favorite pattern, quilted her own stitches and signed her name, creating an enduring memento.

After years of teaching, we are always amazed that each student's quilt emerges as a thoroughly personal expression of herself as she selects colors, patterns and fabrics for a special purpose. One student was making her first quilt for the baby she was carrying. It was filled with favorite prints and colors. While the quilt was being constructed, the pregnancy terminated, bringing grief and sorrow to this young woman. The quilt became a source of comfort: as she stitched each piece, she had quiet time to reflect about the child.

One of the dearest expressions of caring was the quilt top designed with small squares representing the quiltmaker's entire fabric collection. A note was written on the border of the quilt: "Made by Mary Bragdon for Diana McClun. If you need any fabric, I have these."

There are many times when we need praise and recognition, and the quilt becomes the perfect bridge to people who will be impressed with the patterns, the colors, and the time we invested. Even if we don't exhibit in shows or contests, we like our family and friends to give us their approval. The husband of one beginning student kept displaying the unfinished quilt to guests: as the quilt progressed, the praise grew; now this quilt hangs proudly on the wall.

A quilt bridges generations of a family together. Diana grew up in Preston, Idaho, a small town near the Utah border. Her grandmothers, Louisa Nuffer and Ruby Hampton, were both quilters, and each of their quilts tells an autobiographical story. Grandmother Nuffer made her own wool batts and purchased scraps from the Utah Woolen Mills for her utilitarian quilts with dark flannel backs; Grandmother Hampton made beautiful, brightly patched quilts from cotton scraps. From the pieces her mother made for Diana's bridal quilt and for the quilts she sent to Kansas, Illinois and California to celebrate the arrival of each grandchild, it is obvious that she loved color, fabric and ornamentation and was a skilled seamstress.

This same sense of bonding occurred in Laura's family. At an early age she developed an unquenchable thirst for cloth to make doll clothes, from an old sheet or discarded shirt. She can remember spending hours in fabric shops with her mother, who didn't sew, but who encouraged her. This mother-daughter team adored being with each other. During her adolescence, every school sewing class was a step towards understanding the exciting processes of cutting, pinning, picking colors and stitching. By the time she met Diana, Laura had graduated from college and had years of sewing experience. It was in a color class Diana was teaching at her shop, Empty Spools, that they found and shared a common bond. Soon Laura was quilting and teaching classes at Empty Spools, giving every minute to the well-being of the business, helping quilters with problems, choosing colors, and organizing fashion and gallery shows to honor quiltmakers. Laura's quilting friends secretly made a beautiful appliqué and trapunto bridal quilt for her marriage to Bill. However, it was Laura who designed and stitched yards and yards of French lace and Swiss batiste into a magnificent wedding dress. And now there are quilts for her daughters Sara and Molly, quilts for the family and quilts for friends. Those childhood experiences, the stories told to her of her grandmother's sewing expertise and her mother's love and encouragement all built for her a heritage of women that is so much a part of her life.

We both share with you the same joy and love of creativity our ancestors had. Now it's time to do what we do best—detail the construction of a quilt from start to finish, so you too can have the experiences only a quilt can bring.

HOW TO USE *QUILTS! QUILTS!! QUILTS!!!*

Let's take the mystery out of quiltmaking. If you are a beginner, you need to be willing to learn the few—but essential—basics. If you have already made a quilt, you know it requires some diligence and patience (attributes many people think unattainable, yet develop as they become quiltmakers!). But there is no mystery. People who had considered themselves lacking in creativity have produced quilts of great beauty. You can, too!

EVERYTHING YOU NEED TO KNOW IS HERE

Quilts! Quilts!! Quilts!!! deliberately includes patterns that beginning quiltmakers can complete successfully, as well as designs an experienced quiltmaker will enjoy working with. There are popular and traditional patterns—and all the instructions and techniques required to make them.

The patterns are arranged in a progressive sequence, incorporating new designs and utilizing more difficult techniques as you move from the simpler patterns to the more complex. Some patterns require more precise work than others, but with care all can be completed by the quiltmaker who begins with the simpler patterns, moving onward as experience warrants. There are years of joyous quiltmaking within these pages.

You can select one of the patterns and make a quilt or you can make a variety of pattern blocks and incorporate them into a Sampler quilt similar to the examples shown on page 12 and pages 144 to 145. (Choose one you like or make up your own combination of blocks.) Using some of the quick techniques included here, you can complete a quilt in a reasonable period of time and move on to another one that interests you.

SIX STEPS TO SUCCESSFUL QUILTS

This series of steps will help you best use *Quilts! Quilts!! Quilts!!!*

Step 1. Read First Then Quilt
Read through the entire book from start to finish to get an overall idea of the quiltmaking process. Don't jump around. All the important information is not given in the first few pages but developed progressively throughout. Next, re-read the book, spending time on the Practice Exercises. These are intended as learning experiences to familiarize you with basic quiltmaking techniques before you begin your first quilt. (If you are an experienced quiltmaker, you can skip some of these exercises, but we urge you to do the ones involving time-saving techniques.) Instructions for making the quilts assume that you have knowledge of the techniques, including those developed in the Practice Exercises. If you do, you will be happy with your results.

Since this is intended as a workbook, wide margins and spaces for your personal notes have been given. The Table of Contents serves also as an index to the book, with specific page listings. It is conveniently placed at the front for ready reference. In addition, there is a complete index in the back of the book. We have highlighted *Helpful Hints* and *Warnings* we feel are important. You should feel free to highlight other points yourself and add personal observations. Then, you can decide which techniques you feel most comfortable with—quick methods, traditional methods, or a combination of the two.

Step 2. Choose a Pattern

Look through Chapter 1, "Choosing a Pattern." For a positive quilting experience, we recommend that a beginner make one of the quilts requiring only strips (such as *Fence Rail* or *Roman Square*) as a first quilt. Work and become comfortable with its techniques before moving on to patterns with squares, triangles or diamonds. If you are an experienced quiltmaker, choose freely from among the many patterns offered. Remember: the patterns in Chapter 1 are arranged in a progressive sequence.

Step 3. Determine the Size of Your Quilt

Decide on the finished size of the quilt you wish to make. How do you intend to use it? Will it be used on a bed or as a wall hanging? Once you've determined this, turn to the pattern you selected in Chapter 1. There you will find a chart that succinctly gives you the total number of pattern blocks and suggested border widths recommended for the setting and size quilt you wish to make. You will also find convenient fabric requirements for all quilt sizes and settings.

Step 4. Decide on a Color Scheme

For most quiltmakers, this is the most difficult decision. Since we can't see the finished quilt but can only speculate upon what it will look like, this is an especially difficult task for the beginner. Fabric suggestions have been included with each pattern in Chapter 1, and guidelines, exercises and examples are included in Chapter 2, which deals extensively with the color selection process. Take the time to study Chapter 2 and you will create a quilt that is pleasing to you.

Step 5. Prepare Your Fabric

The procedures necessary for preparing your fabric for cutting and sewing are discussed in Chapters 3 and 4. Whether you are experienced or a novice, take the time to treat your fabric with the required care before you begin to cut.

Step 6. Make Your Quilt

Chapters 5 through 10 include step-by-step instructions with diagrams and illustrations of the various techniques required for making the quilts in this book. Study the instructions, work on the Practice Exercises if you have not yet done so and become familiar with the necessary techniques before beginning your quilt.

USING THE PATTERNS

Whenever possible, we have used a 12″ (30 cm) quilt block for the patterns we selected for this book. We've included popular and classic traditional patterns. *Everything you need to know to make every quilt in this book is included here.* Each pattern in this book includes the following:

1. Complete instructions for making the quilt.
2. At least one color photograph of the pattern as an entire quilt.
3. A color diagram of the individual pattern block.
4. A sew-order block which indicates the order in which the individual pieces are sewn together.
5. Fabric requirements for a variety of bed and wall sizes.
6. Suggested fabrics.
7. Techniques required to make the quilt.
8. Template patterns for each individual part of the pattern block. These template patterns can be used for both machine and hand work.

So, remember, there is no mystery. Relax. The more you sew, the more you will know. And the more you will enjoy. *Quilts! Quilts!! Quilts!!!* was created for your enjoyment. And there is no more pleasurable pastime than quiltmaking. It is an elixir for the soul. Happy Quilting!

UNDERSTANDING FABRIC

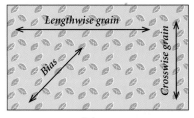

Selvage

Selvage. *The lengthwise finished edges of a woven fabric.*
Grain. *The lengthwise and crosswise threads of a woven fabric used in its construction. The lengthwise grain runs parallel to the selvage edges of the fabric. This has the least amount of stretch. The crosswise grain runs perpendicular to the selvage edges and has a little more stretch.*
Bias. *The diagonal of a woven fabric in which a true 45° angle is formed. The bias has the greatest amount of stretch.*

Fiber content is important when you purchase fabric for your quilts. The content determines the way in which the fabric will respond to manipulation. We strongly recommend that you purchase 100% cotton fabrics. Cotton is strong when wet, irons easily at high temperatures, creases easily, absorbs moisture and wears well. Read the label on the bolt-end of the fabric to determine the fiber content. Quilters need to purchase good-quality, colorfast cotton fabric that is treated with finishes to control shrinkage, resist soil and resist wrinkling.

Not only is the type and quality of the fabric important, but also the printed or woven surface design—and, of course, the color. You must like the fabric; in fact, you should love it and want to live with it. The design should be pleasing to you. Check to see if there is a one-way direction to the design; this will affect the way the fabric will be cut, and you may need to purchase extra fabric to allow for cutting fabrics such as plaids and stripes (whether horizontal, vertical or diagonal). Take a few minutes to analyze the fabric before purchasing it.

The scale of the design and the spaces between the designs (called the background) are also important considerations. Is the design large, medium or small? Is the background area prominent? How will the design look when cut into small pieces? If the design is too widely spaced, you may lose it. Look at the samples on the following pages and keep them in mind when you are shopping.

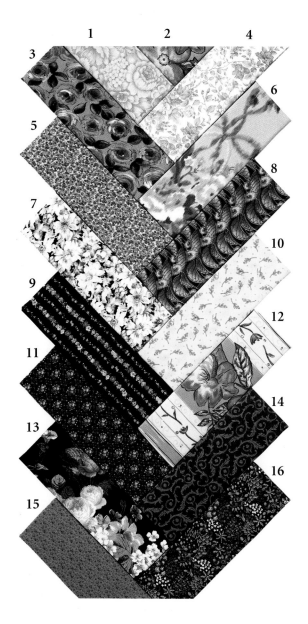

FLORAL FABRICS

Flowers, leaves and grasses, with their wide variety, form one of the largest groups of printed fabrics. Floral prints can be either realistic or stylized. This popular motif has been used since ancient times, symbolizing the beauty of nature with all the splendor of the garden.

1. Monotone, realistic, nondirectional
2. Stylized, large floral packed, nondirectional
3. Stylized, non directional
4. Monotone, realistic, nondirectional, shaded
5. Stylized, multi-colored paisley
6. Realistic warp print, simulated, two directional
7. All over, packed realistic nondirectional
8. Stylized two-directional
9. Floral geometric stripe, two-directional border print
10. Small scale, stylized, tossed, nondirectional
11. Geometric grid, outlining small floral, directional
12. Geometric stripes, stylized flowers, two directional
13. Realistic, large floral, nondirectional
14. Meandering leaves and flowers, monotone, nondirectional
15. Monotone, small scale, basic floral calico, non-directional—smallness gives an illusion of texture
16. All-over, packed small-scale, realistic, nondirectional

Helpful Hints

• Vary the scale of floral motifs from large to very small to give variety and interest to the patterns.

• Monotones (two color floral) help to break up the profusion of colors that most floral color schemes represent by giving the eye a resting place.

• Geometrics such as stripes and plaids make a pleasing companion for florals.

GEOMETRIC FABRICS

Many of the shapes in the quilt block designs in *Quilts! Quilts!! Quilts!!!* are geometric. This ageless category has a long history, and geometric patterns continue to entertain us with seemingly endless variations on a non-representational theme. Geometrics include circles, spirals, stars, squares, rectangles, hexagons, ogees, triangles, diamonds and many other interesting shapes.

1. Squares, painterly, abstract
2. Squares, checkerboard
3. Squares, plaid
4. Squares, windowpane
5. Squares, uneven
6. Circles, painterly, shaded
7. Circles, dots, spirals
8. Circles, pin dots
9. Circles, representing baseballs (making this fabric fall into the conversational category, too)
10. Circles in stripes and triangles
11. Uneven stripes
12. Multi-stripes in various widths
13. Diamond-shape batik
14. Abstract, bold combination of circular diamonds and stripes
15. Ogee
16. Circles, bending and twisting to form cone-like shapes

Helpful Hints

• Geometrics can serve to bind the floral and conversational prints. They add another dimension rather than complicate the design of the block. They also hold the block design together.

• Extra fabric and cutting time are required when using geometrics.

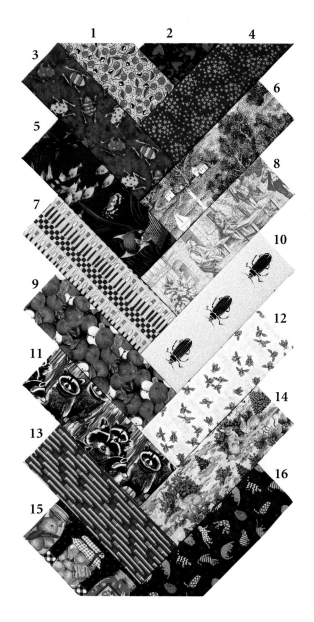

CONVERSATIONAL FABRICS

This category includes motifs that depict real-life people, animals, objects, and scenes. These fabrics are sometimes referred to as novelty prints. Some of the oldest conversational fabrics are the scenic toiles made in France.

1. Fruit, stylized cherries, scattered, all-over, non-directional
2. Hearts, scattered all-over, nondirectional
3. Frogs, stylized, nondirectional
4. Stars, small, all-over, geometric, nondirectional
5. Fish, ocean scene, directional
6. Pointillist nature scene, directional
7. Geometric, striped silverware, directional
8. Toile scene, directional
9. Fruit, apples, all-over, packed, nondirectional
10. Insects, geometric, realistic, two-directional
11. Raccoons, realistic, directional
12. Honeybees, all-over tossed, realistic, nondirectional
13. Pencils, geometric stripes, directional
14. Nature scene, animals, directional
15. Fruit jars, realistic, large, directional
16. Cats, stylized, tossed, nondirectional

Helpful Hints
• All directional and two-directional prints require more fabric and placement time.

• This category establishes a theme or a mood that the quilt-maker wants to depict.

ETHNIC, FOLKLORIC, AND ABSTRACT FABRICS

We have grouped these fabrics together to give you an impression of the enormous range of designs available from countries around the world.

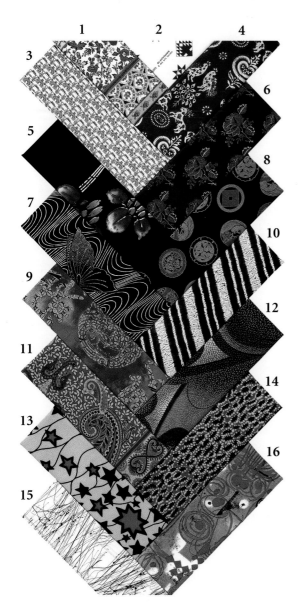

1 French provincial, stripe, floral, conversational
2. French conversational, commemorative
3. German, geometric, conversational, folkloric
4. Dutch, stylized, conversational, folkloric
5. Japanese, stylized, floral
6. German, floral
7. Japanese, geometric, conversational
8. Japanese crests, geometric, floral
9. Javanese batik
10. Japanese diagonal stripe
11. Paisley, provincial, folkloric
12. Dutch, abstract
13. African, conversational, geometric, all-over
14. African, geometric
15. Abstract, line drawing
16. Abstract, painterly, all-over

Helpful Hints

• Many ethnic prints are self-stylizing and are best used that way to keep the mood and feel of the fabric. Small, geometric designs help to break up the boldness of the prints.

• Stripes add dimension to rather than detract from abstract and folkloric designs.

• Many solid or plain batiks are helpful in showcasing design elements in floral and abstract painted fabrics.

EQUIPMENT AND SUPPLIES

1. Graph paper, ⅛″ (0.2 cm) grid
2. Template plastic
3. Protractor
4. C-Thru plastic 1″ × 6″ (3 cm × 15 cm) ruler
5. C-Thru plastic 2″ × 18″ (10 cm × 45 cm) ruler
6. Drafting compass
7. Rotary cutter for template plastic and fabric
8. Pencil sharpener
9. Masking tape
10. Eraser
11. Lead pencils, #2.5 and #3
12. Ultra fine permanent pens, black and red
13. Fabric scissors, 8″ (20 cm)
14. Paper scissors
15. Small scissors
16. Thread clips
17. Rotary cutting mat
18. Rotary cutter for fabric
19. Assorted plastic rulers (with marked 45° angle) 4″ × 4″, 6″ × 12″, 6″ × 6″, 3″ × 18″ (15 cm × 30 cm, 15 cm × 15 cm, 10 cm × 45 cm)
20. Sewing machine
21. Steam iron
22. Even-feed walking foot for sewing machine
23. Steel safety pins, #1
24. Cotton/polyester thread
25. Sewing machine needle, #12, #80
26. Glass-head pins
27. Tape measure
28. Needles, #9, #10, and #12 Betweens
29. Cotton thread
30. Needle threader
31. Seam ripper
32. Quilting thread
33. Reducing glass
34. Cotton darning needle, #1
35. Finger cots
36. Needle grabber
37. Thimble
38. Bag balm
39. Artist's soft pencils, multi colors
40. Fabric marking pencils, white, gray, and silver
41. Quilting hoop or frame
42. Quilting design template
43. Batting
44. Fusible web with paper back
45. Freezer paper

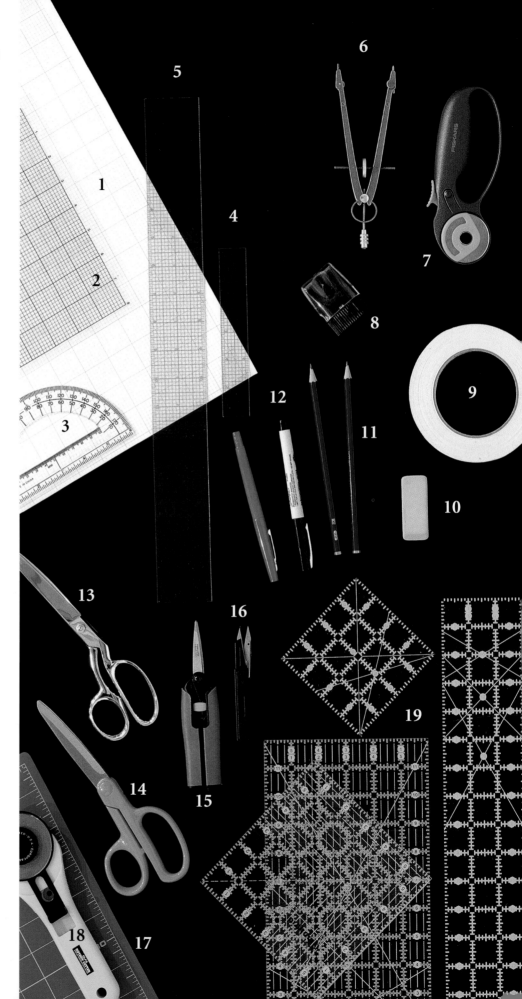

Barbara's Sampler, Barbara Wilson

Chapter 1

CHOOSING A PATTERN

 The patterns in this chapter are organized in a progressive fashion; the easiest patterns come first. Beginning quiltmakers are urged to start with one of the patterns that require only strip piecing: *Fence Rail, Roman Square,* or *Nine-Patch.*

Fabric. We have listed generous amounts of fabric in the charts. Our experience tells us that there are few things in quiltmaking as frustrating as nearing the end of a quilt project only to discover that you are short of an essential fabric. Use the extra fabric that will be left over to begin—or replenish—your scrap bag for future quilt projects.

Cutting charts. It is important that you cut your fabric *in the order listed in the charts, so that you do not cut into a length you will need elsewhere.*

Hand or machine work. We have listed template numbers and quick-cutting methods with each pattern. Thus, these pattern instructions can be used for either hand or machine work.

Borders. We have given suggested border widths in the cutting charts. These are only suggestions. If you feel confident enough, determine your own borders and their widths. This may, however, change the amount of border and backing fabric required.

Quilt sizes. All are given as width × length: 61″ × 90″ (155 cm × 229 cm).

Dimensions. All are rounded *up* to the nearest whole number.

Metric measurements. All measurements are supplied both in Imperial (inches/yards) and metric (centimeters/meters). If you are working in metric, your finished blocks and quilts will be a slightly different size from those of a quilter working in Imperial measurements, for example, a finished block will measure 12″ or 30 cm. This is because each pattern has been completely redrafted in metric to make the book easier to use. Use a 0.75 cm seam allowance.

ROMAN SQUARE

Diana McClun and Laura Nownes, quilted by Anna Venti

Block size: 4½″ (12 cm)
Techniques: Quick-cutting, strip piecing, or Template 2M
Setting: Diagonal
Fabric suggestions: Variety of scraps, twice as many darks as lights

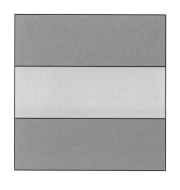

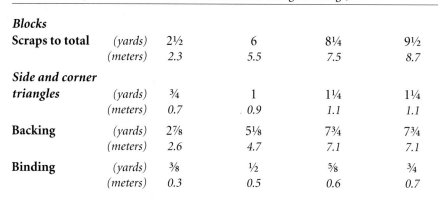

		Crib/Wall	Twin	Double/Queen	King
Finished size	*(inches)*	45 × 57	70 × 89	89 × 96	108 × 89
	(centimeters)	119 × 153	187 × 238	238 × 255	289 × 238
Blocks set		7 × 9	11 × 14	14 × 15	17 × 14
Pieced blocks		111	284	392	446
Side triangles		28	46	54	58

FABRIC *(Based on 42″ to 44″/106 cm to 112 cm selvage to selvage)*

		Crib/Wall	Twin	Double/Queen	King
Blocks					
Scraps to total	*(yards)*	2½	6	8¼	9½
	(meters)	2.3	5.5	7.5	8.7
Side and corner					
triangles	*(yards)*	¾	1	1¼	1¼
	(meters)	0.7	0.9	1.1	1.1
Backing	*(yards)*	2⅞	5⅛	7¾	7¾
	(meters)	2.6	4.7	7.1	7.1
Binding	*(yards)*	⅜	½	⅝	¾
	(meters)	0.3	0.5	0.6	0.7

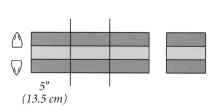

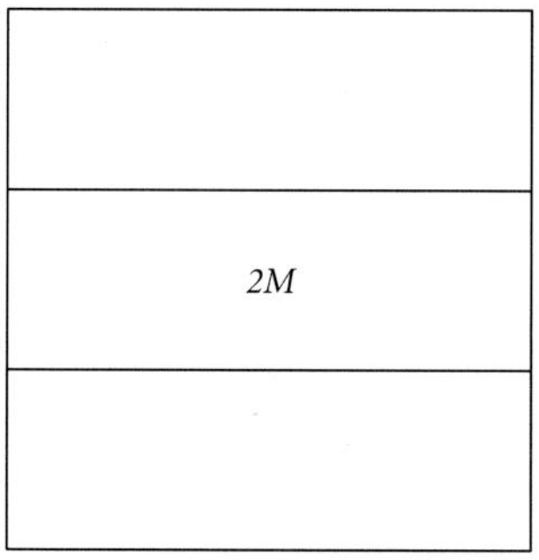

Cutting

CUTTING

		Crib/Wall	Twin	Double/Queen	King
Blocks					
2″ (5.5 cm) strips		42	108	147	168
Side triangles					
8½″ (22 cm) squares		7	12	14	15
Corner triangles					
6″ (15 cm) squares		2	2	2	2
Backing	*(lengths)*	2	2	3	3

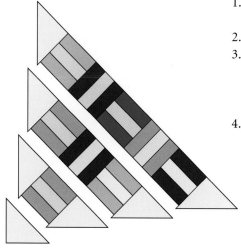

5″
(13.5 cm)

Step 2

CONSTRUCTION

1. Sew a variety of different combinations of sets. Each set consists of one light between two dark strips.
2. Cut each set apart every 5″ (13.5 cm), as shown.
3. To make the side triangles, cut each 8½″ (22 cm) square in quarters diagonally. To make the corner triangles, cut the 6″ (15 cm) squares in half diagonally. *Note:* Both the side and corner triangles are cut too big to allow for straightening the quilt top edges.
4. Sew the blocks, side triangles, and corner triangles together in a diagonal set, as shown.

Step 4

FENCE RAIL

Diana McClun and Laura Nownes, quilted by Kathy Sandbach

Block size: 12″ (30 cm)
Techniques: Quick-cutting and strip piecing or Template 2E
Setting: Straight
Fabric suggestions: Two combinations of six fabrics each for blocks and pieced border, graduated from light to dark

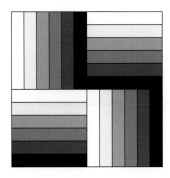

		Crib/Wall	Twin	Double/Queen	King
Finished size	*(inches)*	42 × 54	66 × 90	84 × 96	108 × 96
	(centimeters)	105 × 135	165 × 225	210 × 240	270 × 240
Blocks set		3 × 4	5 × 7	6 × 7	8 × 7
Total blocks		12	35	42	56

FABRIC *(Based on 42″ to 44″/106 cm to 112 cm selvage to selvage)*

Blocks and borders

		Crib/Wall	Twin	Double/Queen	King
Twelve fabrics each	*(yards)*	⅜	¾	⅞	1
	(meters)	0.3	0.7	0.8	0.9
Backing	*(yards)*	1¾	5¼	5¾	8½
	(meters)	1.6	4.8	5.3	7.8
Binding	*(yards)*	⅜	⅝	⅝	¾
	(meters)	0.3	0.6	0.6	0.7

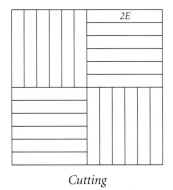

Cutting

CUTTING

Blocks
		Crib/Wall	Twin	Double/Queen	King
1½″ (4 cm) strips, twelve fabrics each		8	24	28	38
Pieced border		20	30	24	32
Width	*(inches)*	3½	3½	6½	6½
	(centimeters)	9	9	16.5	16.5
Length	*(inches)*	9½	10½	14½	12½
	(centimeters)	24	26.5	36.5	31.5
Backing	*(lengths)*	1	2	2	3

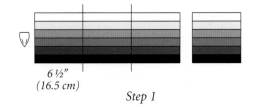

6½″
(16.5 cm)

Step 1

CONSTRUCTION

1. Sew six strips together sequenced from light to dark, to make each of two combinations of each set. Cut the sets apart every 6½″ (16.5 cm), as shown.
2. Block sew order: see diagram.
3. Sew the blocks together in a straight set.
4. Join the border pieces, then attach to complete the quilt top. *Note:* For all sizes except the double/queen, attach the top and bottom borders first, then the side borders. For the double/queen, attach the side borders first.

Helpful Hint: See the *Fence Rail* Practice Exercise in Chapter 5 for help.

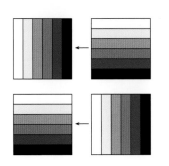

Step 2

LOG CABIN

Diana McClun and Laura Nownes, quilted by Kathy Sandbach

Block size: 12″ (30 cm)
Techniques: Quick-cutting or Templates 1D, 2A, 2B, 2C, 2D, 2E, 2F, 2G, 2H, 2J, 7B, and 7C
Setting: Straight
Fabric suggestions: One fabric for center squares; a variety of fabrics for strips

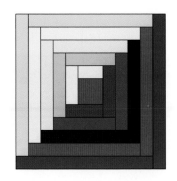

	Crib/Wall	Twin	Double/Queen	King
Finished size (inches)	48 × 60	72 × 84	84 × 96	108 × 96
(centimeters)	120 × 150	180 × 210	210 × 240	270 × 240
Blocks set	4 × 5	6 × 7	7 × 8	9 × 8
Total blocks	20	42	56	72

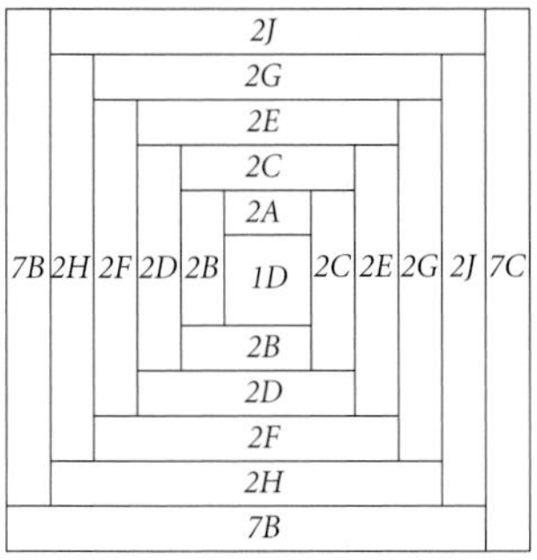

FABRIC (Based on 42″ to 44″/106 cm to 112 cm selvage to selvage)

		Crib/Wall	Twin	Double/Queen	King
Centers					
Scraps to total	(yards)	¼	¼	⅜	½
	(meters)	0.2	0.2	0.3	0.5
Strips					
Scraps to total	(yards)	4	7	9	12
	(meters)	3.7	6.4	8.2	11
Backing	(yards)	3	5	5⅝	8½
	(meters)	2.7	4.6	5.1	7.8
Binding	(yards)	⅜	½	⅝	¾
	(meters)	0.3	0.5	0.6	0.7

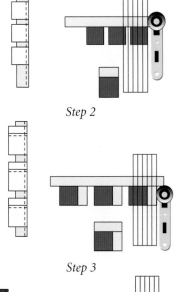

Cutting

CUTTING

		Crib/Wall	Twin	Double/Queen	King
Centers					
2½″ (6.5 cm) strips		2	3	4	5
Strips	(inches)	1½	1½	1½	1½
	(centimeters)	4	4	4	4
Backing	(lengths)	2	2	2	3

Helpful Hint: Organize several different block combinations before cutting.

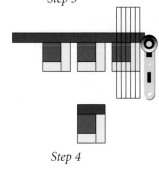

Step 2

Step 3

Step 4

Step 5

CONSTRUCTION

1. Cut the center strips into 2½″ (6.5 cm) squares.
2. With right sides together, sew the center squares (1D) to a strip of the first light fabric (2A). Press toward the first light fabric. Cut the units apart as shown.
3. With right sides together, sew the units formed in Step 2 to another strip of the first light fabric (2B). Press toward the first light fabric. Cut as shown.
4. With right sides together, sew the units formed in Step 3 to a strip of the first dark fabric (2B). Press toward the first dark fabric. Cut as shown.
5. Add another strip of the first dark fabric and cut to make units as shown.
6. Using Steps 3 to 4 as a guide, sew the remaining strips to the units as follows: second light, second dark, third light, third dark, fourth light, fourth dark, fifth light, fifth dark. Note that each fabric is used in two positions.
7. Sew the blocks together in a straight set, using the photograph as a guide.

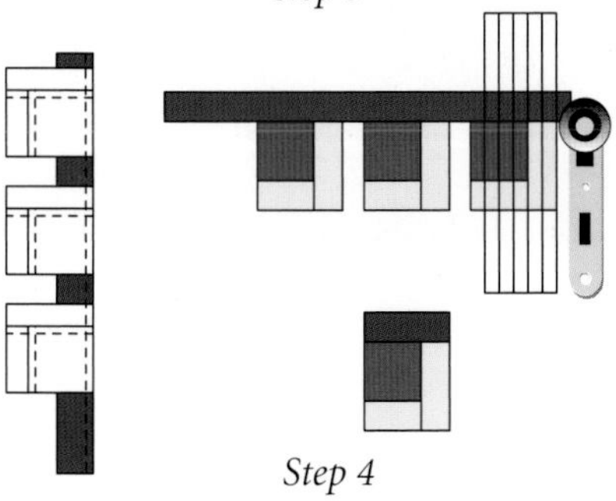

Helpful Hint: All blocks are constructed in the same manner. You can vary the arrangement to create different designs.

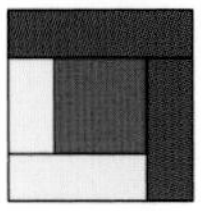

FOUR-PATCH

Dena Canty, quilted by Kathy Sandbach

Block size: 8″ (20 cm)
Techniques: Quick-cutting and strip piecing or Templates 1B, 1D, and 1H
Setting: Straight
Fabric suggestions: Scraps and a border fabric to complement your pieced blocks

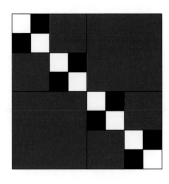

	Crib/Wall	Twin	Double/Queen	King
Finished size (inches)	56 × 56	72 × 88	88 × 88	104 × 104
(centimeters)	140 × 140	180 × 220	220 × 220	260 × 260
Blocks set	6 × 6	8 × 10	10 × 10	12 × 12
Total blocks	36	80	100	144

FABRIC (Based on 42″ to 44″ /106 cm to 112 cm selvage to selvage)

		Crib/Wall	Twin	Double/Queen	King
Four-Patch units					
Scraps to total (yards)		1	2	2½	3¾
(meters)		0.9	1.8	2.3	3.4
Plain blocks					
Scraps to total (yards)		1¾	3¾	4¾	6¾
(meters)		1.6	3.4	4.3	6.2
Border (yards)		1¾	2½	2½	3
(meters)		1.6	2.3	2.3	2.7
Backing (yards)		3½	5¼	7¾	9
(meters)		3.2	4.8	7.1	8.2
Binding (yards)		¾	⅝	¾	¾
(meters)		0.7	0.6	0.7	0.7

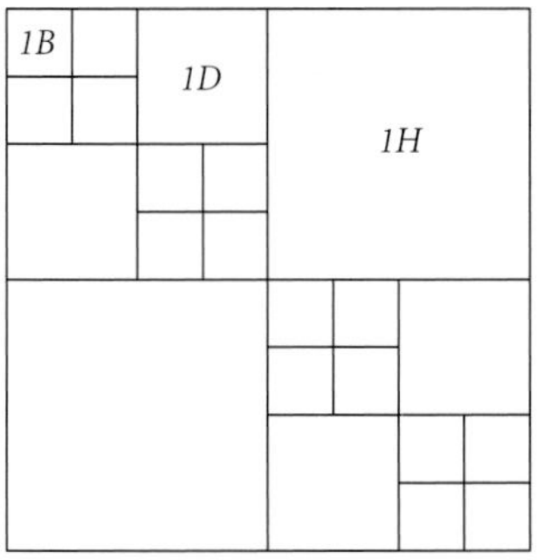

CUTTING

		Crib/Wall	Twin	Double/Queen	King
Four-Patch units					
1B: 1½″ (4 cm) strips		22	46	58	84
Plain blocks					
1D: 2½″ (6.5 cm) strips		9	20	25	36
1H: 4½″ (11.5 cm) strips		8	18	23	32
Border (inches)		4½	4½	4½	4½
(centimeters)		11.5	11.5	11.5	11.5
Backing (lengths)		2	2	3	3

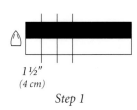

Cutting

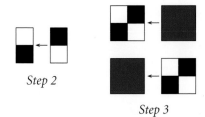

1½″
(4 cm)

Step 1

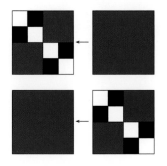

Step 2

Step 3

Step 4

CONSTRUCTION

1. Join the 1B strips together in pairs. Cut the sets apart every 1½″ (4 cm), as shown. Cut the 1D strips into 2½″ (6.5 cm) squares, and cut the 1H strips into 4½″ (11.5 cm) squares.
2. Unit construction: see diagram.
3. Block sew order: see diagram. Note the placement of the light squares in the four-patch units.
4. Sew the blocks together in a straight set.
5. Attach the border to complete the quilt top.

Helpful Hint: Lay out all of the blocks before sewing, starting from the center and working out, to ensure correct placement of the four-patch units.

NINE-PATCH

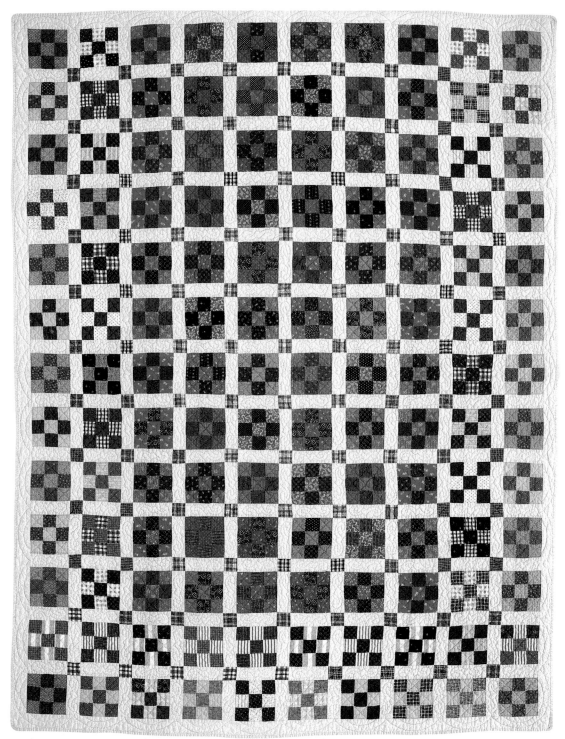

Maker unknown, collection of Margaret Peters

Block size: 4½″ (12 cm)
Techniques: Quick-cutting and strip piecing or Template 1C
Setting: Straight with sashing and posts
Fabric suggestions: Light-colored fabric for sashing and borders, scraps for Nine-Patches, and post fabric to complement the pieced blocks

		Crib/Wall	Twin	Double/Queen	King
Finished size	*(inches)*	45 × 63	69 × 93	87 × 87	105 × 93
	(centimeters)	118 × 166	182 × 246	230 × 230	278 × 246
Blocks set		7 × 10	11 × 15	14 × 14	17 × 15
Light blocks (outer)		46	74	76	86
Dark blocks (inner)		24	91	120	169

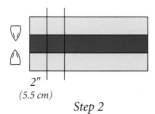

Cutting

FABRIC *(Based on 42″ to 44″/106 cm to 112 cm selvage to selvage)*

		Crib/Wall	Twin	Double/Queen	King
Light fabric					
Sashing, borders *(yards)*		2	2¾	3¼	4¼
	(meters)	1.8	2.5	3	3.9
Nine-Patch blocks					
Scraps to total	*(yards)*	2	4	4¾	6½
	(meters)	1.8	3.7	4.3	5.9
Posts					
Scraps to total	*(yards)*	¼	½	⅝	¾
	(meters)	0.2	0.5	0.6	0.7
Backing	*(yards)*	3	5¼	7¾	8¼
	(meters)	2.7	4.8	7.1	7.5
Binding	*(yards)*	⅜	½	⅝	¾
	(meters)	0.3	0.5	0.6	0.7

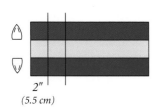

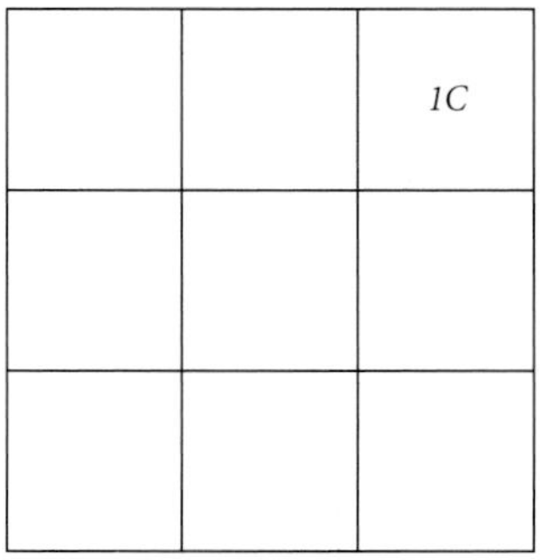

2″
(5.5 cm)

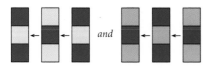

2″
(5.5 cm)

Step 2

CUTTING

		Crib/Wall	Twin	Double/Queen	King
Light fabric					
Borders (cut lengthwise)					
	(inches)	2½	2½	2½	2½
	(centimeters)	6.5	6.5	6.5	6.5
Sashing: 2″ (5.5 cm) strips		16	38	46	64
Nine-Patch blocks					
2″ (5.5 cm) strips		33	72	84	117
Posts					
2″ (5.5 cm) squares		54	140	169	230
Backing	*(lengths)*	2	2	3	3

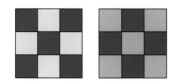

Step 3

CONSTRUCTION

1. Cut sashing strips into 2″ × 5″ (5.5 cm × 13.5 cm) pieces.
2. For Nine-Patches, sew several different combinations of strips and cut every 2″ (5.5 cm), as shown. Refer to the chart for the exact number of light and dark blocks needed.
3. Block sew order: see diagram.
4. Sew the blocks together in a straight set, joining with sashing and posts.
5. Attach the borders to complete the quilt top. Trim any extra length from the border strips.

Step 4

DOUBLE NINE-PATCH

Rosalee Sanders

Block size: 9″ (22.5 cm)
Techniques: Quick-cutting, strip piecing, and half-square triangles, or Templates 1B, 1F, and 4R (pieced border)
Setting: Straight, with alternate blocks
Fabric suggestions: One light, one medium, and one dark

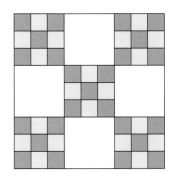

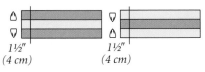

Cutting

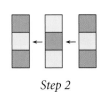

Step 1

	Crib/Wall	Twin	Double/Queen	King
Finished size *(inches)*	51 × 51	71 × 89	89 × 89	95 × 95
(centimeters)	127 × 127	172 × 223	223 × 223	238 × 238
Blocks set	5 × 5	7 × 7	9 × 9	9 × 9
Pieced blocks	13	25	41	41
Alternate blocks	12	24	40	40

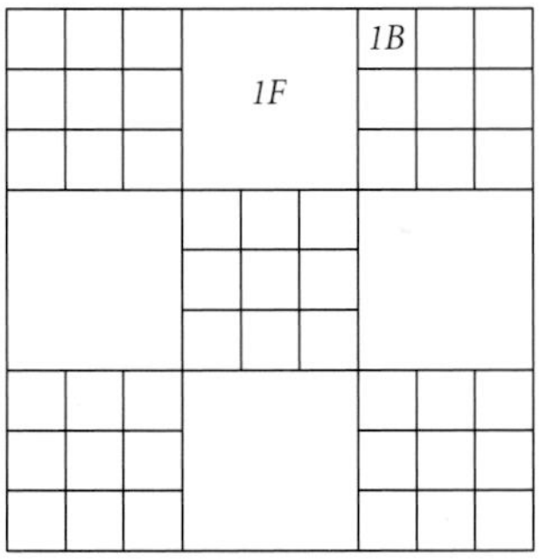

FABRIC *(Based on 42″ to 44″/106 cm to 112 cm selvage to selvage)*

	Crib/Wall	Twin	Double/Queen	King
Light fabric (includes borders) *(yards)*	2¼	5¼	6½	6½
(meters)	2.1	4.8	5.9	5.9
Pieced blocks and sawtooth border				
Medium fabric *(yards)*	¾	2	2¾	2¾
(meters)	0.7	1.8	2.5	2.5
Dark fabric *(yards)*	¾	2¼	3¼	3¼
(meters)	0.7	2.1	3	3
Backing *(yards)*	2¾	4½	7¾	8½
(meters)	2.5	4.1	7.1	7.8
Binding *(yards)*	⅜	½	⅝	¾
(meters)	0.3	0.5	0.6	0.7

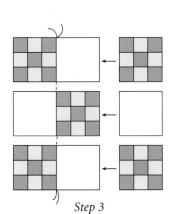

Step 2

Step 3

Step 4

CUTTING

	Crib/Wall	Twin	Double/Queen	King
Light fabric				
Inner and outer borders (cut lengthwise) *(inches)*	1½	2	2	3½
(centimeters)	4	5.3	5.3	9
Alternate blocks				
9½″ (24 cm) squares	12	24	40	40
1F: 3½″ (9 cm) strips	5	9	14	14
Medium fabric				
1B: 1½″ (4 cm) strips	10	18	30	30
4R: 1⅞″ (5 cm) strips	5	7	9	9
Dark fabric				
1B: 1½″ (4 cm) strips	12	23	37	37
4R: 1⅞″ (5 cm) strips	5	7	9	9
Backing *(lengths)*	2	2	3	3

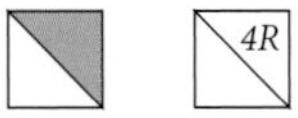

CONSTRUCTION

1. Cut the 1F strips into 3½″ (9 cm) squares. Sew two combinations of 1B strips and cut apart every 1½″ (4 cm), as shown.
2. Nine-Patch unit construction: see diagram.
3. Sew order: see diagram.
4. Sawtooth border: cut all the strips into 1⅞″ (5 cm) squares, then in half diagonally. Make half-square triangle units from medium and dark 4R pieces.
5. Attach the borders to complete the quilt top.

DOUBLE NINE-PATCH VARIATION

Diana McClun and Laura Nownes, quilted by Kathy Sandbach

Block size: 12¾″ (32.5 cm)
Techniques: Quick-cutting and strip piecing, or Templates 1B and 1F
Setting: Straight
Fabric suggestions: Scraps for Nine-Patches and plain squares. Two fabrics for large triangles

		Crib/Wall	Twin	Double/Queen	King
Finished size	*(inches)*	58 × 58	71 × 84	84 × 97	97 × 97
	(centimeters)	*147 × 147*	*179 × 211*	*211 × 243*	*243 × 243*
Blocks set		3 × 3	4 × 5	5 × 6	6 × 6
Total blocks		9	20	30	36

FABRIC *(Based on 42″ to 44″/106 cm to 112 cm selvage to selvage)*

		Crib/Wall	Twin	Double/Queen	King
Nine-Patch units					
Scraps to total	*(yards)*	1	1⅝	2¼	2¾
	(meters)	*0.9*	*1.5*	*2.1*	*2.5*
Plain squares					
Scraps to total	*(yards)*	⅜	¾	1¼	1½
	(meters)	*0.3*	*0.7*	*1.1*	*1.4*
Large triangles					
Each of two fabrics	*(yards)*	½	1	1⅜	1¾
	(meters)	*0.5*	*0.9*	*1.3*	*1.6*
Border print fabric					
Four 10½″ (27 cm)	*(yards)*	1¾	2¾	3	3
repeats*	*(meters)*	*1.6*	*2.5*	*2.7*	*2.7*
Backing	*(yards)*	3	4¾	8	8¾
	(meters)	*2.7*	*4.3*	*7.3*	*8*
Binding	*(yards)*	½	½	¾	¾
	(meters)	*0.3*	*0.5*	*0.7*	*0.7*

* Applies only for fabrics with a repeating pattern

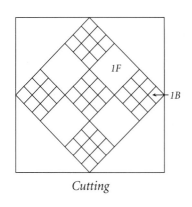

Cutting

CUTTING

		Crib/Wall	Twin	Double/Queen	King
Nine-Patch units					
1½″ (4 cm) strips		16	33	49	60
Plain squares					
3½″ (9 cm) strips		3	7	10	12
Large triangles					
7¾″ (19.5 cm)					
squares, each		9	20	30	36
Border	*(inches)*	10½	10½	10½	10½
	(centimeters)	*27*	*27*	*27*	*27*
Backing	*(lengths)*	2	2	3	3

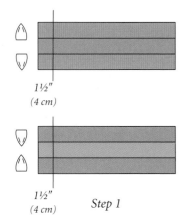

1½″
(4 cm)

1½″
(4 cm)

Step 1

CONSTRUCTION

1. Cut the 1F strips into 3½″ (9 cm) squares. Sew several different combinations of 1B strips and cut apart every 1½″ (4 cm), as shown.
2. Nine-Patch unit construction: see diagrams.
3. Block sew order: see diagram.
4. Cut the squares for the large triangles in half diagonally; the triangles will be a little too large. Then attach them to the blocks. Trim the excess and straighten the edges.
5. Sew the blocks together in a straight set, alternating fabrics used for the large triangles.
6. Attach the borders to complete the quilt top.

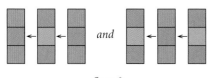

and

Step 2

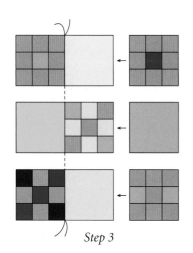

Step 3

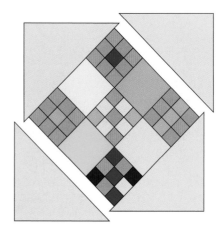

Step 4

HOPSCOTCH NINE-PATCH

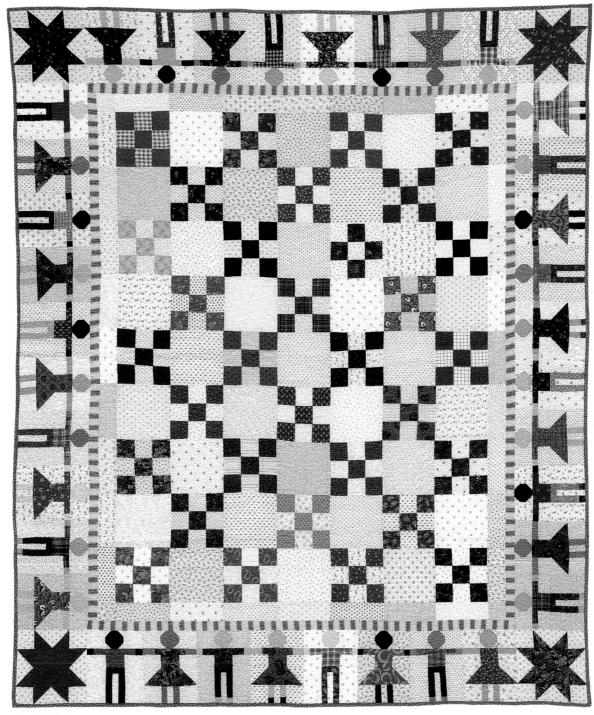

Dorie Whipple

Nine-Patch and alternate block size: 4½″ (11.4 cm) **Kids block size:** 4½″ × 6″ (11.4 cm × 15 cm)
Sawtooth Star block size: 6″ (15 cm)
Techniques: Quick-cutting, strip piecing and double half-square triangle technique, or Templates 1A, 1C, 1F, 1J, 2K, 2L, 2M, 3A, 3B, 3D, 4J, 4Q, and 5G
Setting: Straight
Fabric suggestions: Variety of scraps

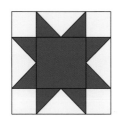

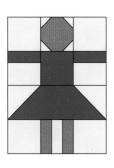

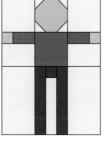

	Crib/Wall	Twin	Double/Queen	King
Finished size *(inches)*	48 × 57	75 × 93	84 × 93	102 × 93
(centimeters)	122 × 145	191 × 236	213 × 236	259 × 236
Blocks set	7 × 9	13 × 17	15 × 17	19 × 17
Nine-Patch blocks	32	111	128	162
Alternate blocks	31	110	127	161
Kids blocks	36	64	68	76
Sawtooth Star blocks	4	4	4	4

FABRIC *(Based on 42″ to 44″/106 cm to 112 cm selvage to selvage)*

	Crib/Wall	Twin	Double/Queen	King
Light fabric				
Scraps to total *(yards)*	1	3½	4	5
(meters)	0.9	3.2	3.7	4.6
Nine-Patches, Kids, and Sawtooth Star blocks				
Scraps to total *(yards)*	1	3½	4	5
(meters)	0.9	3.2	3.7	4.6
Second inner border				
(yards)	¼	⅜	⅜	⅜
(meters)	0.2	0.3	0.3	0.3
Backing *(yards)*	3	5½	5½	8¼
(meters)	2.7	5	5	7.5
Binding *(yards)*	⅜	½	⅝	¾
(meters)	0.3	0.5	0.6	0.7

CUTTING

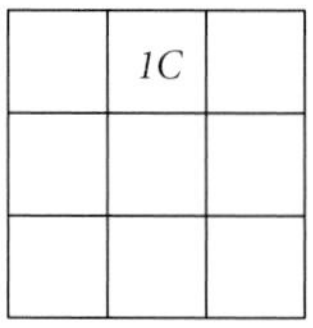

	Crib/Wall	Twin	Double/Queen	King
Nine-Patch blocks				
Light: 2″ (5.1 cm) strips	7	22	25	31
Dark: 2″ (5.1 cm) strips	8	27	31	39
Alternate blocks				
5″ (12.9 cm) squares	31	110	127	161
First inner border				
2″ × 5″ (5.3 cm × 12.9 cm)	32	60	64	72
2″ (5.1 cm) squares	4	4	4	4
Second inner border				
(inches)	1¼	1¼	1¼	1¼
(centimeters)	3.2	3.2	3.2	3.2
Kids blocks, boys ★				
4T: 1″ (2.8 cm) squares	4	4	4	4
3C : 1″ × 3″ (2.8 cm × 7.8 cm)	1	1	1	1
2K: 1½″ × 2″ (3.4 cm × 5.3 cm)	2	2	2	2
1C: 2″ (5.3 cm) squares	2	2	2	2

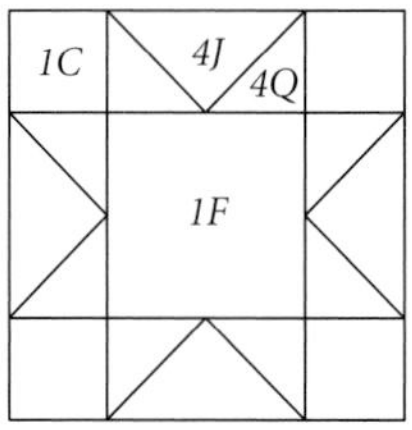

Nine-Patch block   Sawtooth Star block

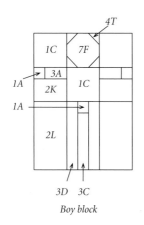

Boy block

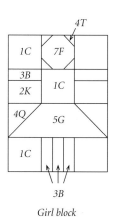

Girl block

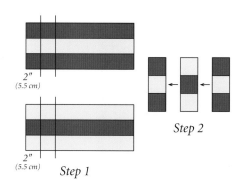

2″
(5.5 cm)

Step 1

Step 2

	Crib/Wall	Twin	Double/Queen	King
2L: 2″ × 3½″ (5.3 cm × 9 cm)	2	2	2	2
7F (head): 2″ (5.3 cm) squares	1	1	1	1
3A (shirt): 1″ × 1½″ (2.8 cm × 3.4 cm)	2	2	2	2
1C (shirt): 2″ (5.3 cm) squares	1	1	1	
1A (pants): 1″ (2.8 cm) squares	1	1	1	1
3D: 1″ × 3½″ (2.8 cm × 9 cm)	2	2	2	2
1A (hands): 1″ (2.8 cm) squares	2	2	2	2
Kids blocks, girls *				
4T: 1″ (2.8 cm) squares	4	4	4	4
1C: 2″ (5.3 cm) squares	4	4	4	4
3B: 1″ × 2″ (2.8 cm × 5.3 cm)	1	1	1	1
2K: 1½″ × 2″ (4 cm × 5.3 cm)	2	2	2	2
4Q: 2″ (5.3 cm) squares	6	6	6	6
7F (head): 2″ (5.3 cm) squares	1	1	1	1
3B (dress): 1″ × 2″ (2.8 cm × 5.3 cm)	2	2	2	2
1C: 2″ (5.3 cm) squares	1	1	1	1
5G: 2″ × 5″ (5.3 cm × 12.8 cm)	1	1	1	1
3B (legs): 1″ × 2″ (2.8 cm × 5.3 cm)	2	2	2	2
Sawtooth Star blocks *				
1C: 2″ (5.3 cm) squares	4	4	4	4
4J: 2″ × 3½″ (5.3 cm × 9 cm)	4	4	4	4
4Q: 2″ (5.3 cm) squares	8	8	8	8
1F: 3½″ (9 cm) squares	1	1	1	1

*All numbers are pieces per block

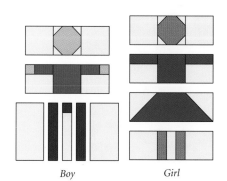

Step 3

Boy   *Girl*

Step 4

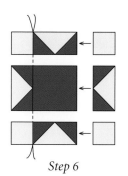

Step 6

CONSTRUCTION

1. For Nine-Patches, sew several different combinations of strips using the 2″ (5.3 cm) strips. Cut apart every 2″ (5.3 cm), as shown.
2. Nine-Patch block construction: see diagram.
3. Unit construction for Kids blocks: see diagrams. *Note:* Use double half-square triangles to attach the background squares to the head and skirt fabric.
4. Kids block sew order: see diagrams.
5. For Sawtooth Star blocks, make double half-square triangle units.
6. Star block sew order: see diagram.
7. Sew the Nine-Patch and alternate blocks together in a straight set, beginning and ending with Nine-Patches in the corners.
8. Sew pieces and attach the pieced inner border, then the second inner border.
9. Attach the Kids block and Sawtooth Star border to complete the quilt top.

PINWHEEL

Diana McClun and Laura Nownes, quilted by Kathy Sandbach

Block size: 6″ (15 cm)
Techniques: Quick-cutting and double half-square triangles, or Templates 1K (alternate block) and 4N
Setting: Diagonal
Fabric suggestions: Light and dark fabrics for pieced blocks; a variety of fabrics for alternate blocks

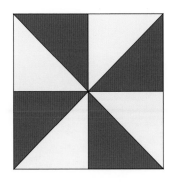

	Crib/Wall	Twin	Double/Queen	King
Finished size *(inches)*	42 × 60	68 × 85	85 × 93	102 × 102
(centimeters)	*106 × 148*	*169 × 210*	*210 × 231*	*252 × 252*
Blocks set	5 × 7	8 × 10	10 × 11	12 × 12
Pieced blocks	35	80	110	144

FABRIC *(Based on 42″ to 44″/106 cm to 112 cm selvage to selvage)*

		Crib/Wall	Twin	Double/Queen	King
Pinwheel blocks					
Light fabric	*(yards)*	1	2	2⅝	3⅜
	(meters)	*0.9*	*1.8*	*2.4*	*3.1*
Dark fabric	*(yards)*	1	2	2⅝	3⅜
	(meters)	*0.9*	*1.8*	*2.4*	*3.1*
Alternate blocks and side/corner triangles					
Scraps to total	*(yards)*	1½	2½	4	5
	(meters)	*1.4*	*2.3*	*3.7*	*4.6*
Backing	*(yards)*	3¾	5	5½	9
	(meters)	*3.4*	*4.6*	*5*	*8.2*
Binding	*(yards)*	⅜	½	¾	¾
	(meters)	*0.3*	*0.5*	*0.7*	*0.7*

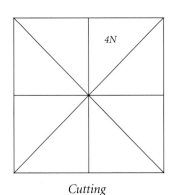

Cutting

CUTTING

	Crib/Wall	Twin	Double/Queen	King
Pinwheel blocks				
3⅞″ (10 cm) squares of lights and darks, each	70	160	220	288
Alternate blocks				
6½″ (16.5 cm) squares	24	63	90	121
Side triangles				
10½″ (27 cm) squares	5	8	10	11
Corner triangles				
9″ (23 cm) squares	2	2	2	2
Backing *(lengths)*	2	2	2	3

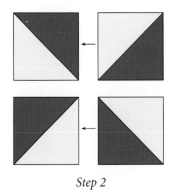

Step 2

CONSTRUCTION

1. Cut squares for Pinwheel blocks and corner triangles in half diagonally; cut squares for side triangles into quarters diagonally. Sew half-square triangle units from the light and dark triangles for the Pinwheel blocks. Press seams open to reduce bulk. Check for accuracy; each unit should measure 3½″ (9 cm).
2. Block sew order: see diagram.
3. Sew the Pinwheel blocks, alternate blocks, and side and corner triangles together in a diagonal set as shown.
4. Trim the excess fabric to straighten the edges to within ½″ (1.5 cm) of the corners of the Pinwheel blocks.

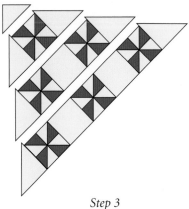

Step 3

OCEAN WAVES

Gai Perry

Block size: 12″ (30 cm)
Techniques: Quick-cutting or Templates 1K and 4U
Setting: Diagonal
Fabric suggestions: Dark for background, scraps for triangles

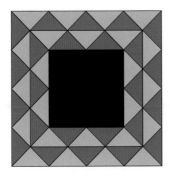

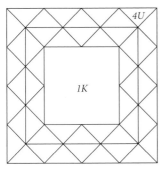

Cutting

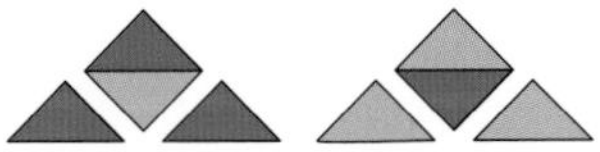

Step 2

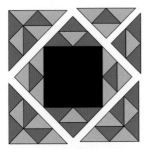

Step 3

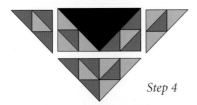

Step 4

	Crib/Wall	Twin	Double/Queen	King
Finished size *(inches)*	44 × 44	67 × 84	84 × 84	101 × 101
(centimeters)	*108 × 108*	*167 × 209*	*209 × 209*	*251 × 251*
Whole blocks	4	17	24	40
Half-blocks	8	14	16	20

FABRIC *(Based on 42″ to 44″/106 cm to 112 cm selvage to selvage)*

		Crib/Wall	Twin	Double/Queen	King
Dark fabric **(includes borders)**					
	(yards)	1½	3½	3¾	4½
	(meters)	1.4	3.2	3.4	4.1
Triangles					
Scraps to total	*(yards)*	2	4	5¼	8¼
	(meters)	1.8	3.7	4.8	7.5
Light middle border					
	(yards)	¼	2¾	3	3¼
	(meters)	0.2	2.5	2.7	3
Backing	*(yards)*	3¾	5¼	6¼	9
	(meters)	3.4	4.8	5.8	8.2
Binding	*(yards)*	⅜	½	⅝	¾
	(meters)	0.3	0.5	0.6	0.7

CUTTING

		Crib/Wall	Twin	Double/Queen	King
Dark fabric					
1K: 6½″ (16.5 cm) strips		2	3	6	7
9¾″ (25 cm) squares		2	3	3	4
Inner border	*(inches)*	1½	2	1½	1½
	(centimeters)	4	5.3	4	4
Outer border	*(inches)*	3	5	6	6
	(centimeters)	7.8	12.8	15.3	15.3
Dark and light triangles					
4U: 3″ (7.9 cm) strips		14	42	55	86
Middle border	*(inches)*	2	2½	2	2
	(centimeters)	5.3	6.5	5.3	5.3
Backing	*(lengths)*	2	2	2	3

CONSTRUCTION

1. Cut 1K strips into 6½″ (16.5 cm) squares. Cut 9¾″ (25 cm) squares for the half-blocks in quarters diagonally. Cut 4U strips into 3″ (7.9 cm) squares. Then cut the squares into quarters diagonally.
2. Unit construction: see diagrams. Make six each for whole blocks and three each for half blocks.
3. Block sew order: see diagram.
4. Half-block sew order: see diagram.
5. Assembly: when joining blocks, be certain to match the light triangles of one block to the dark triangles of the next, as shown.
6. Attach borders to complete the quilt top.

Step 5

WILD GOOSE CHASE

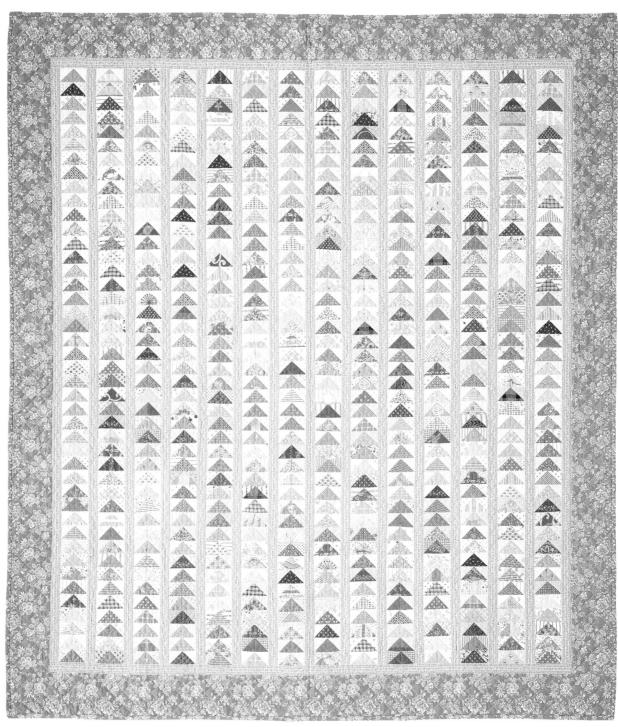

Pat Callis

Unit size: 1½″ × 3″ (3.8 cm × 7.5 cm)

Setting: Vertical

Techniques: Quick-cutting and double half-square triangles or Templates 4J and 4Q

Fabric suggestions: A variety of light fabrics for small triangles and medium to dark fabrics for large triangles. Narrow border-printed fabric for sashing. Fabric for the outside border that complements your finished units

		Crib/Wall	Twin	Double/Queen	King
Finished size	(inches)	40 × 54	67 × 88	85 × 94	101 × 94
	(centimeters)	100 × 135	168 × 220	212 × 235	253 × 235
Rows		8	12	16	22
Units per row		30	45	48	48
Total units		240	540	768	960

FABRIC *(Based on 42″ to 44″/106 cm to 112 cm selvage to selvage)*

		Crib/Wall	Twin	Double/Queen	King
Small triangle					
Scraps to total*	(yards)	1⅜	2⅝	3½	5¼
	(meters)	1.3	2.4	3.2	4.8
Large triangle					
Scraps to total*	(yards)	1⅜	3	4¼	5¾
	(meters)	1.3	2.7	3.9	5.3
Sashing and inner border	(yards)	1½	2⅛	2¼	2½
	(meters)	1.4	1.9	2.1	2.3
Outer border and binding	(yards)	1⅞	2¾	3	3⅜
	(meters)	1.7	2.5	2.7	3.1
Backing	(yards)	1¾	5⅛	8¼	8¼
	(meters)	1.6	4.7	7.5	7.5

*Less fabric is needed if template cutting rather than quick-cutting

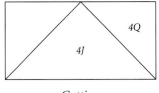

Cutting

CUTTING

		Crib/Wall	Twin	Double/Queen	King
4J: 3½″ (9 cm) strips		12	26	37	51
4Q: 2″ (5.3 cm) strips		23	52	74	101
Sashing: 1½″ (4 cm) strips		7	11	15	21
Inner border	(inches)	1½	1½	1½	1½
	(centimeters)	4	4	4	4
Outer border	(inches)	4	9½	10½	10½
	(centimeters)	12	24.5	27	27
Backing	(lengths)	1	2	3	3

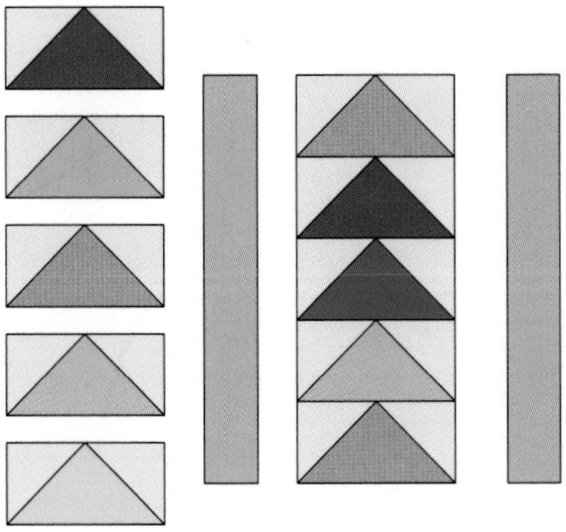

CONSTRUCTION

1. Cut 4J strips into 2″ x 3½″ (5.3 cm x 9 cm) rectangles and 4Q strips into 2″ (5.3 cm) squares.
2. Make double half-square triangle units. See page 104 for help.
3. Sew the units together to form vertical rows.
4. Sew sashing strips between the rows. See instructions for sashing in Chapter 7 for help in keeping the units straight when attaching the sashing strips.
5. Attach the inside and the outside borders to complete the quilt top.

Steps 3 and 4

WILD GOOSE CHASE VARIATION

Diana McClun and friends, quilted by Barbara Wilson

Block size: 12″ (30 cm)
Techniques: Quick-cutting and double half-square triangles or Templates 1F, 1K, 4U, and 4Q
Setting: Straight
Fabric suggestions: Scraps

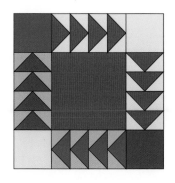

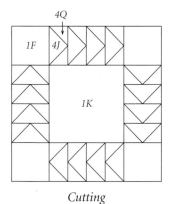

Cutting

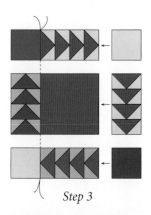

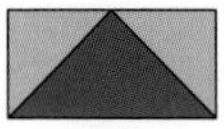

Step 2

Step 3

Step 4

	Crib/Wall	Twin	Double/Queen	King
Finished size *(inches)*	48 × 60	72 × 84	84 × 96	108 × 96
(centimeters)	120 × 150	180 × 210	210 × 240	270 × 240
Blocks set	4 × 5	6 × 7	7 × 8	9 × 8
Total blocks	20	42	56	72

FABRIC *(Based on 42″ to 44″/106 cm to 112 cm selvage to selvage)*

Blocks				
Scraps to total *(yards)*	4⅞	9½	12¾	16¼
(meters)	4.3	8.7	11.7	14.9
Backing *(yards)*	3	5	5⅝	8½
(meters)	2.7	4.6	5.1	7.8
Binding *(yards)*	⅜	½	⅝	¾
(meters)	0.3	0.5	0.6	0.7

CUTTING

1K: 6½″ (16.5 cm) strips	4	7	10	12
1F: 3½″ (9 cm) strips	7	14	19	24
4Q: 2″ (5.3 cm) strips	31	64	86	110
4J: 3½″ (9 cm) strips	16	32	43	55
Backing *(lengths)*	2	2	2	3

CONSTRUCTION

1. Cut 1K strips into 6½″ (16.5 cm) squares, 1F strips into 3½″ (9 cm) squares, 4Q strips into 2″ (5.3 cm) squares, and 4J strips into 2″ × 3½″ (5.3 cm × 9 cm) pieces.
2. Make double half-square triangle units, as shown.
3. Block sew order: see diagram.
4. Sew the blocks together in a straight set, alternating the placement of the light and dark corners, as shown in the photograph.

SAWTOOTH STAR

Alex Anderson

Block size: 4″ (10 cm)
Techniques: Quick-cutting and double half-square triangles, or Templates 1B, 1D, 4K, and 4R
Setting: Straight with sashing
Fabric suggestions: Dark background and scraps for stars

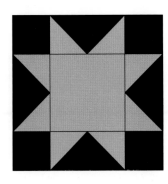

	Wall	Twin	Double/Queen	King
Finished size *(inches)*	59 × 59	69 × 91	86 × 95	104 × 95
(centimeters)	*144 × 144*	*175 × 231*	*218 × 241*	*264 × 241*
Blocks set	10 × 10	12 × 17	16 × 18	20 × 18
Total blocks	100	204	288	360

FABRIC *(Based on 42″ to 44″/106 cm to 112 cm selvage to selvage)*

	Wall	Twin	Double/Queen	King
Background, sashing, outside border *(yards)*	4⅜	7¼	9¼	11
(meters)	4	6.6	8.5	10.1
Stars and pieced inside border				
Scraps to total *(yards)*	2¼	4¼	5⅝	7
(meters)	2.1	3.9	5.1	6.4
Backing *(yards)*	3½	5⅜	8⅜	9
(meters)	3.2	4.9	7.7	8.2
Binding *(yards)*	½	½	⅝	¾
(meters)	0.5	0.5	0.6	0.7

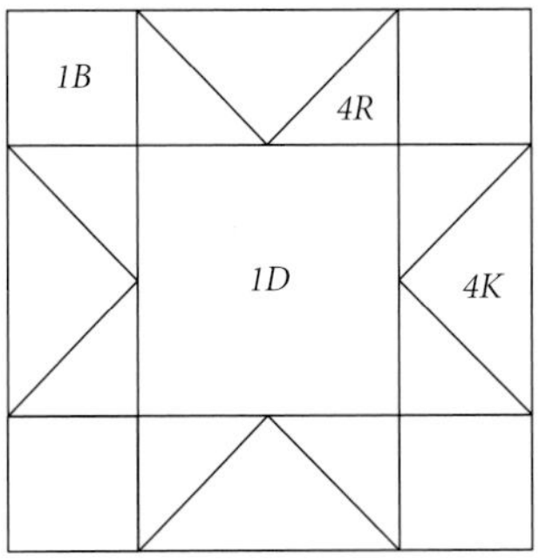

CUTTING

	Wall	Twin	Double/Queen	King
Background fabric **Inside border and (cut lengthwise) Sashing and inner border:**				
1″ (2.8 cm) strips	8	11	9	8
Outer border:				
6″ (15.2 cm) strips	2	2	2	1
Then cut crossgrain:				
1B: 1½″ (4 cm) strips	31	68	77	80
4K: 2½″ (6.5 cm) strips	31	68	77	80
Star fabric				
4R: 1½″ (4 cm) strips	29	59	83	103
1D: 2½″ (6.5 cm) strips	7	13	18	23
Pieced middle border strips: varying widths from ⅞″ to 1¼″ (2.2 cm to 3.2 cm)	24	24	30	36
Backing *(lengths)*	2	2	3	3

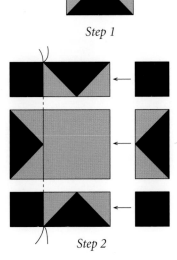

Cutting

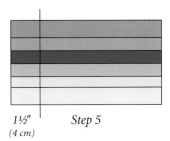

Step 1

Step 2

1½″
(4 cm)   *Step 5*

CONSTRUCTION

1. Cut the 1B and 4R strips into 1½″ (4 cm) squares, the 4K strips into 1½″ × 2½″ (4 cm × 6.5 cm) pieces, and the 1D strips into 2½″ (6.5 cm) squares. Make double half-square triangle units with the 4R and 4K pieces.
2. Block sew order: see diagram.
3. Cut sashing strips to lengths as needed. Join with star blocks in a straight set.
4. Attach inner border.
5. For middle border, sew strips together in sets of six. Cut every 1½″ (4 cm).
6. Sew the cut strips together to the required length for each side of your quilt.
7. Attach outer border.

ATTIC WINDOWS

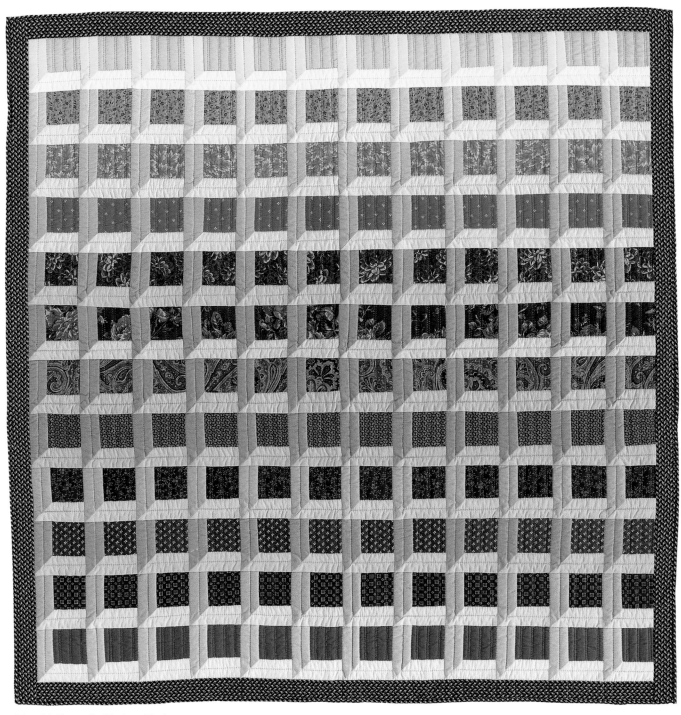

Diana McClun, quilted by Anna Venti

Block size: 12″ (30 cm)

Techniques: Quick-cutting or Template 1E, and Template 7D

Setting: Straight

Fabric suggestions: Fabrics graduated in color around the color wheel for window panes. Two shades of each color for the sills and sides. Fabric that complements your finished blocks for the border

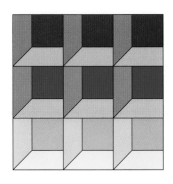

	Crib/Wall	Twin	Double/Queen	King
Finished size *(inches)*	51 × 51	75 × 87	87 × 87	94 × 99
(centimeters)	*128 × 128*	*188 × 218*	*218 × 218*	*248 × 248*
Blocks set	4 × 4	6 × 7	7 × 7	8 × 8
Total blocks	16	42	49	64

FABRIC *(Based on 42″ to 44″/106 cm to 112 cm selvage to selvage)*

		Crib/Wall	Twin	Double/Queen	King
Window panes					
Scraps to total	*(yards)*	1⅛	2⅜	3⅛	4⅜
	(meters)	*1*	*2.2*	*2.9*	*4*
Window sills					
Scraps to total	*(yards)*	1¼	3	3¾	5¼
	(meters)	*1.1*	*2.7*	*3.4*	*4.8*
Window sides					
Scraps to total	*(yards)*	1¼	3	3¾	5¼
	(meters)	*1.1*	*2.7*	*3.4*	*4.8*
Border and binding					
	(yards)	1¾	2¾	3¼	3⅜
	(meters)	*1.6*	*2.5*	*3*	*3.1*
Backing	*(yards)*	3⅜	5	8⅝	8⅝
	(meters)	*3.1*	*4.6*	*7.9*	*7.9*

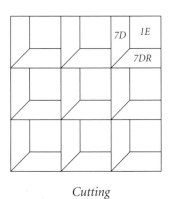

Cutting

CUTTING

		Crib/Wall	Twin	Double/Queen	King
1E: 3″ (7.8 cm) strips		11	27	36	53
7D and 7DR*:					
2″ (5.5 cm) strips, each		18	48	63	92
Border	*(inches)*	2	2	2	2
	(centimeters)	5.3	5.3	5.3	5.3
Backing	*(lengths)*	2	2	3	3

*R = reverse template on fabric

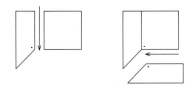

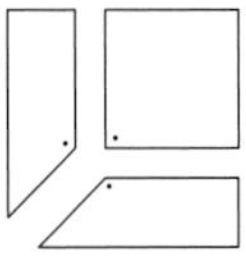

Step 2

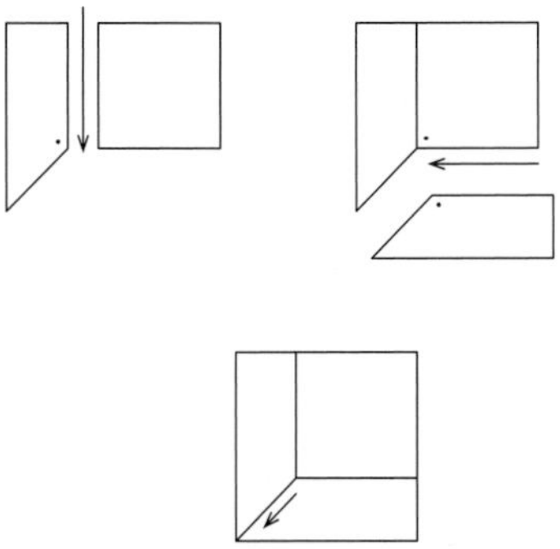

CONSTRUCTION

1. Cut 1E strips into 3″ (7.8 cm) squares. Use the template to cut the angles on the 7D and 7DR strips.
2. The technique required to construct the block by machine is called "Y-seam construction." You must not stitch into the seam allowance at the crook of the Y. *Helpful Hint:* Indicate the stopping point with a dot on the template and the wrong side of each appropriate fabric piece, as shown in the diagram.
3. Unit construction: stitch in the direction indicated by the arrows.
4. Block sew order: see diagram.
5. Sew blocks together in a straight set.
6. Attach border to complete the quilt top.

Step 3

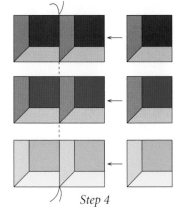

Step 4

SPOOL

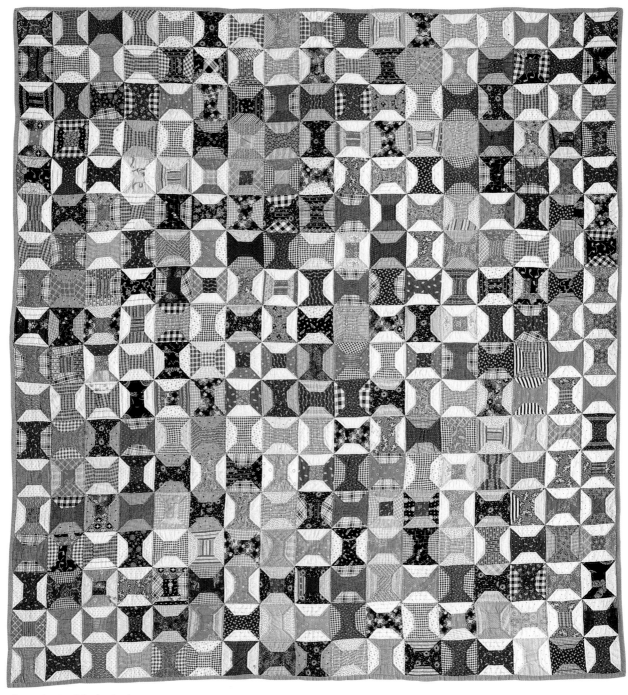

Samantha Ann Wheeler Curtis, 1910

Block size: 6″ (15 cm)
Techniques: Quick-cutting or Template 1D, and Template 7A
Setting: Straight
Fabric suggestions: Variety of scraps

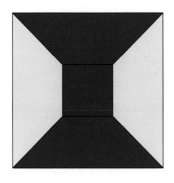

	Crib/Wall	Twin	Double/Queen	King
Finished size *(inches)*	48 × 60	66 × 90	84 × 96	108 × 102
(centimeters)	*120 × 150*	*165 × 225*	*210 × 240*	*270 × 255*
Blocks set	8 × 10	11 × 15	14 × 16	18 × 17
Total blocks	80	165	224	306

FABRIC *(Based on 42″ to 44″/106 cm to 112 cm selvage to selvage)*

	Crib/Wall	Twin	Double/Queen	King
Background				
Scraps to total *(yards)*	1½	3⅛	4	5½
(meters)	*1.4*	*2.9*	*3.7*	*5*
Spools				
Scraps to total *(yards)*	2	4	5½	7
(meters)	*1.8*	*3.7*	*5*	*6.4*
Backing *(yards)*	3⅞	5½	8⅝	9⅝
(meters)	*3.5*	*5*	*7.9*	*8.8*
Binding *(yards)*	⅜	½	¾	¾
(meters)	*0.3*	*0.5*	*0.7*	*0.7*

CUTTING

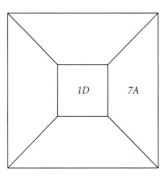

Cutting

	Crib/Wall	Twin	Double/Queen	King
Background				
7A: 2½″ (6.5 cm) strips	20	42	57	77
Spools				
1D: 2½″ (6.5 cm) strips	5	11	15	20
7A: 2½″ (6.5 cm) strips	20	42	57	77
Backing *(lengths)*	2	2	3	3

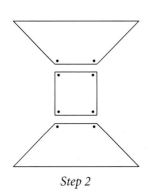

Step 2

CONSTRUCTION

1. Cut the 1D strips into 2½″ (6.5 cm) squares.
2. Use the template to cut the angles on the 7A strips.
3. The technique required to construct the block by machine is called "Y-seam construction." You must not stitch into the seam allowance at the crook of the Y. *Helpful Hint:* Indicate the stopping point with a dot on the template and the wrong side of each appropriate fabric piece as indicated in the diagram.
4. Sew order: stitch in the direction indicated by the arrows.
5. Sew the blocks together in a straight set, alternating the direction of the spools, as shown in the photograph.

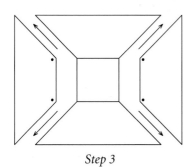

Step 3

MADISON HOUSE

Diana McClun and Laura Nownes, quilted by Kathy Sandbach

House block size: 12″ (30 cm)

Tree block size: 6″ × 12″ (15 cm × 30 cm)

Techniques: Quick-cutting and double half-square triangles, or Templates 1L, 1M, 2A, 2E, 3E, 3G, 3H, 3J, 3L, 3M, 4F, 4N, 4P, 5C, 5D, 5E, 5F, and 7C

Setting: Straight

Fabric suggestions: Variety of fabrics for sky, houses, and trees

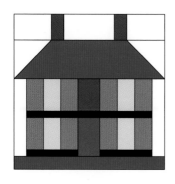

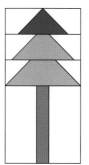

	Crib/Wall	Twin	Double/Queen	King
Finished size *(inches)*	54 × 51	72 × 96	84 × 96	108 × 111
(centimeters)	135 × 128	180 × 240	225 × 240	270 × 278
Total rows	3	6	6	7
House blocks per row	3	4	5	6
Tree blocks per row	2	3	4	5

FABRIC *(Based on 42″ to 44″/106 cm to 112 cm selvage to selvage)*

		Crib/Wall	Twin	Double/Queen	King
Background and pieced borders					
Scraps to total	*(yards)*	1¼	3¼	4	5
	(meters)	1.1	3	3.7	4.6
Houses					
Scraps to total	*(yards)*	2¼	3½	4½	6
	(meters)	2	3.2	4.1	5.5
Trees					
Scraps to total	*(yards)*	¼	⅝	¾	1
	(meters)	0.2	0.6	0.7	0.9
Dark fabric for pieced border					
Scraps to total	*(yards)*	⅜	¾	⅞	1
	(meters)	0.3	0.7	0.8	0.9
Horizontal sashing					
(cut lengthwise)	*(yards)*	1⅝	2⅛	2⅜	3⅛
	(meters)	1.5	1.9	2.2	2.9
Backing	*(yards)*	3⅛	5⅝	5⅝	9⅝
	(meters)	2.9	5.1	5.1	8.8
Binding	*(yards)*	⅜	⅝	¾	¾
	(meters)	0.3	0.6	0.7	0.7

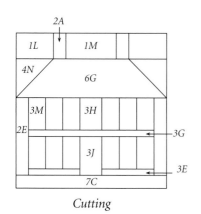

Cutting

CUTTING

House blocks

	Crib/Wall	Twin	Double/Queen	King
Background				
2E: 1½″ × 6½″ (4 cm × 16.5 cm)	18	48	60	84
1L: 2½″ × 3½″ (6.5 cm × 9 cm)	18	48	60	84
1M: 2½″ × 4½″ (6.5 cm × 11.5 cm)	9	24	30	42
4N: 3½″ (9 cm) squares	18	48	60	84
Houses				
2A: 1½″ × 2½″ (4 cm × 6.5 cm)	18	48	60	84
6G: 3½″ × 12½″ (9 cm × 31.5 cm)	9	24	30	42

	Crib/Wall	Twin	Double/Queen	King
Balconies				
1″ (2.8 cm) strips	5	12	15	21
Then cut:				
3E: 1″ × 4⅝″ (2.8 cm × 11.7 cm)	18	48	60	84
3G: 1″ × 10½″ (2.8 cm × 26.5 cm)	9	24	30	42
3M (front): 1⅞″ × 13″ (4.9 cm × 34 cm)	18	48	60	84
3M (windows): 1⅞″ × 13″ (4.9 cm × 34 cm)	9	24	30	42
7C: 1½″ × 12½″ (4 cm × 31.5 cm)	9	24	30	42
3H: 2¼″ × 3″ (6.7 cm × 7.7 cm)	9	24	30	42
3J: 2¼″ × 3½″ (6.7 cm × 9 cm)	9	24	30	42
Tree blocks				
Background				
5D: 2½″ × 3½″ (6.5 cm × 9 cm)	12	36	48	70
5C: 2½″ × 3″ (6.5 cm × 7.8 cm)	12	36	48	70
4P: 2½″ (6.5 cm) squares	12	36	48	70
3L: 3″ × 6½″ (7.8 cm × 16.5 cm)	12	36	48	70
Trees				
4F: 2½″ × 4½″ (6.5 cm × 11.5 cm)	6	18	24	35
5F: 2½″ × 5½″ (6.5 cm × 14 cm)	6	18	24	35
5E: 2½″ × 6½″ (6.5 cm × 16.5 cm)	6	18	24	35
2E: 1½″ × 6½″ (4 cm × 16.5 cm)	6	18	24	35
Horizontal sashing strips	3	6	6	7
(inches)	3½	3½	3½	3½
(centimeters)	9	9	9	9
Pieced border				
Backgrounds and dark fabric:				
1½″ (4 cm) strips, each	7	17	19	23
Backing *(lengths)*	2	2	2	3

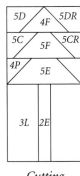

Cutting

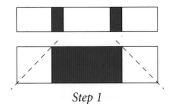

Step 1

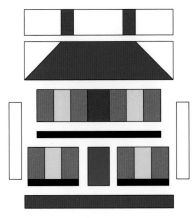

3"
(7.8 cm)

Step 2

CONSTRUCTION

1. Unit construction for houses: see diagrams.
2. Sew the house front strips and window strips together in sets, then cut them apart every 3″ (7.8 cm), as shown.
3. Sew order: see diagram.
4. Unit construction for trees: see diagrams.
5. Sew order: see diagram.
6. Sew the house and tree blocks together in rows. Join the rows with horizontal sashing strips.
7. For the pieced border, sew a variety of strips together in sets, then cut them apart every 3½″ (9 cm), as shown.
8. Attach the pieced borders to complete the quilt top.

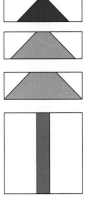

Step 3

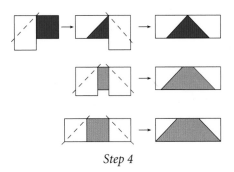

Step 4

Step 5

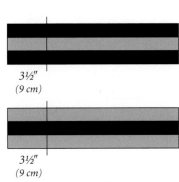

3½"
(9 cm)

3½"
(9 cm)

Step 7

PINE TREE

Laura Nownes and friends, quilted by Kathy Sandbach

Block size: 12″ (30 cm)

Techniques: Quick-cutting and half-square triangles, or Templates 1C, 4L, 4N, 4Q, and 8E, and Template 5B

Fabric suggestions: Background and trunk fabrics; scraps for leaves; and two fabrics for alternate blocks and side and corner triangles

	Crib/Wall	Twin	Double/Queen	King
Finished size *(inches)*	51 × 51	68 × 85	85 × 85	102 × 102
(centimeters)	*126 × 126*	*168 × 210*	*210 × 210*	*252 × 252*
Blocks set	2 × 2	3 × 4	4 × 4	5 × 5
Tree blocks	4	12	16	25
Alternate blocks	9	20	25	36

FABRIC *(Based on 42″ to 44″/106 cm to 112 cm selvage to selvage)*

Tree blocks				
Light background *(yards)*	¾	1⅛	1½	2¼
(meters)	*0.7*	*1*	*1.4*	*2.1*
Trunks *(yards)*	⅜	½	⅝	⅞
(meters)	*0.3*	*0.5*	*0.6*	*0.8*
Leaves				
Light scraps to total *(yards)*	⅝	1½	1¾	2½
(meters)	*0.6*	*1.4*	*1.6*	*2.3*
Dark scraps to total *(yards)*	⅝	1½	2	2⅞
(meters)	*0.6*	*1.4*	*1.8*	*2.4*
Alternate blocks				
Inner blocks, side and corner triangles *(yards)*	1½	2½	2¾	4¼
(meters)	*1.4*	*2.3*	*2.5*	*3.9*
Outer blocks *(yards)*	1⅛	1¾	2¼	2⅝
(meters)	*1*	*1.6*	*2.1*	*2.4*
Backing *(yards)*	3¼	5	5	9
(meters)	*3*	*4.6*	*4.6*	*8.2*
Binding *(yards)*	⅜	½	⅝	¾
(meters)	*0.3*	*0.5*	*0.6*	*0.7*

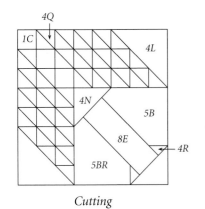

Cutting

CUTTING

Light background				
1C: 2″ (5.3 cm) strips	1	2	3	4
4N: 3⅞″ (10 cm) strips	1	1	1	2
4L: 5⅜″ (13.8 cm) strips	1	2	3	4
5B and 5BR*: 6⅞″ (17.5 cm) strips	1	2	3	5
Trunks				
4R: 1⅞″ (5 cm) strips	1	1	1	2
4N: 3⅞″ (10 cm) strips	1	1	1	2
8E: 2⅝″ (6.9 cm) strips	1	2	3	5
Leaves				
4Q: 2⅜″ (6.3 cm) strips, dark	7	20	26	40
2⅜″ (6.3 cm) strips, light	6	17	23	36

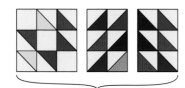

Make one each per block

Make two per block

Step 4

Make one per block

Step 5

Step 6

	Crib/Wall	Twin	Double/Queen	King
Alternate blocks				
Inner blocks:				
12½″ (31.5 cm) strips	1	2	3	6
Side triangles:				
19″ (48.5 cm) strips	1	2	2	3
Corner triangles:				
10″ (25.5 cm) strips	2	2	2	2
Outer blocks:				
12½″ (31.5 cm) strips	3	5	6	7
Backing *(lengths)*	2	2	2	3

R = reverse template on fabric

CONSTRUCTION

1. Tree blocks: Cut 1C strips into 2″ (5.3 cm) squares. Cut 4N strips into 3⅞″ (10 cm) squares, 4L strips into 5⅜″ (13.8 cm) squares, and 5B strips into 6⅞″ (17.5 cm) squares; cut in half diagonally. Use the template to mark and cut the angles for the 5B triangles. *Note:* Half are cut reversed. Cut the 4R strips into 1⅞″ (5 cm) squares and the 4N strips into 3⅞″ (10 cm) squares; cut in half diagonally. Cut the 8E strips into 2⅝″ × 6⅞″ (6.9 cm × 17.7 cm) pieces. Cut the 4Q strips into 2⅜″ (6.3 cm) squares, then cut in half diagonally.

2. Alternate blocks and side/corner triangles: Cut the inner and outer block strips into 12½″ (31.5 cm) squares. Cut the side triangle strips into 19″ (48.5 cm) squares, then cut into quarters diagonally. Cut the corner triangle strips into 10″ (25.5 cm) squares, then cut in half diagonally.

3. Make 24 half-square triangle units per block.

4. Unit construction: see diagrams.

5. Assemble the trunk units, as shown.

6. Block sew order: see diagram.

7. Sew the tree blocks, alternate blocks, and side and corner triangles together in a diagonal set. *Note:* Both the side and corner triangles are cut too big to allow for strengthening the quilt top edges.

BEAR'S PAW

The River City Quilt Guild, quilted by Miriam Patsworth

Block size: 12″ (30 cm)
Techniques: Quick-cutting and half-square triangles or Templates 2P, 2Q, 2T, 3N, and 4A
Setting: Diagonal with alternate blocks
Fabric suggestions: Light and dark contrast

	Crib/Wall	Twin	Double/Queen	King
Finished size (inches)	47 × 64	68 × 85	85 × 85	98 × 98
(centimeters)	*116 × 158*	*168 × 210*	*210 × 210*	*242 × 242*
Blocks set	2 × 3	3 × 4	4 × 4	5 × 5
Pieced blocks	6	12	16	25

FABRIC *(Based on 42″ to 44″/106 cm to 112 cm selvage to selvage)*

		Crib/Wall	Twin	Double/Queen	King
Light	*(yards)*	3	4	6½	7
	(meters)	*2.7*	*3.7*	*5.9*	*6.4*
Dark, including binding	*(yards)*	2	3	4	4½
	(meters)	*1.8*	*2.7*	*3.7*	*4.1*
Backing	*(yards)*	3⅞	4¾	5¾	8½
	(meters)	*3.5*	*4.3*	*5.3*	*7.8*

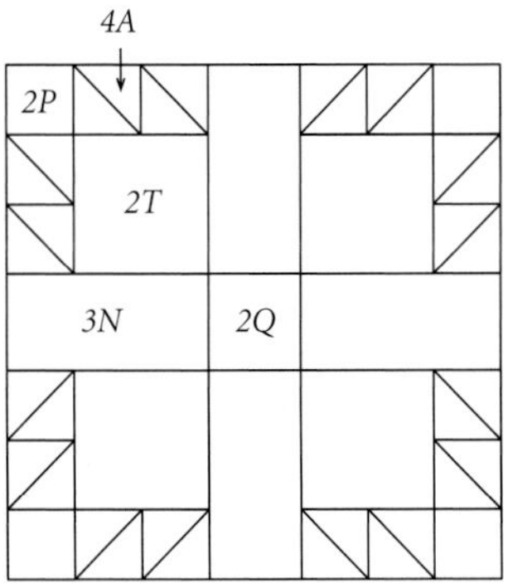

Cutting

CUTTING

	Crib/Wall	Twin	Double/Queen	King
Light fabric				
Pieced blocks and border				
2P: 2⅛″ (5.5 cm) strips	2	3	5	6
4A: 2½″ (6.5 cm) strips	6	10	17	20
3N: 5⅜″ (13.5 cm) strips	2	4	6	7
Alternate blocks				
12½″ (31.5 cm) squares	2	6	9	16
Side triangles				
19″ (48.5 cm) squares	2	3	3	4
Corner triangles				
10″ (25.5 cm) squares	2	2	2	2
Middle border *(inches)*	3¾	5½	5½	3¾
(centimeters)	*9.5*	*14*	*14*	*9.5*
Dark fabric				
2T: 3¾″ (9.5 cm) strips	2	4	7	9
2Q: 2¾″ (7.5 cm) strips	1	1	2	2
4A: 2½″ (6.5 cm) strips	6	10	17	20
Corner blocks for inner and outer sawtooth borders, eight each *(inches)*	2⅛	2⅛	2⅛	2⅛
(centimeters)	*5.5*	*5.5*	*5.5*	*5.5*
Backing *(lengths)*	2	2	2	3

Title   Gourmet
             tortillas: exotic
             and traditional
             tortilla dishes
Item ID: 340510000134
             97
Due   1/25/2012
Title   Wise women :
             a celebration of
             their insights,
             courage, and
             beauty
Item ID.   340510000135
             98
Due   1/25/2012
Title   Quilts! quilts!!
             quilts!!! the
             complete guide
             to quiltmaking
Item ID   340510000135
             27
Due.   1/25/2012
Title   Favorite Brand
             Name
             Recipes : Kids
             4 Books in 1
             Breakfast,
             Lunch, Snacks,
             Dinner
Item ID   340510000208
             89
Due: 1/25/2012

```
**********************************
         ***
```
Sag. Chipp Tribal Library
1/4/2012 1:53:28   989-775-4519
      PM
```
**********************************
         ***
```

Title: Gourmet
                tortillas : exotic
                and traditional
                tortilla dishes
Item ID: 340510000134
                97
Due: 1/25/2012
Title: Wise women :
                a celebration of
                their insights,
                courage, and
                beauty
Item ID: 340510000135
                98
Due: 1/25/2012
Title: Quilts! quilts!!
                quilts!!! : the
                complete guide
                to quiltmaking
Item ID: 340510000135
                27
Due: 1/25/2012
Title: Favorite Brand
                Name
                Recipes : Kids
                4 Books in 1
                Breakfast,
                Lunch, Snacks,
                Dinner
Item ID: 340510000208
                69
Due: 1/25/2012

Make four each per block

Step 2

Step 3

CONSTRUCTION

1. Cut the 2T strips into 3¾″ (9.5 cm) squares, and the 2P strips into 2⅛″ (5.5 cm) squares. Cut the 2Q strips into 2¾″ (7.5 cm) squares. Cut all 4A strips into 2½″ (6.5 cm) squares, then cut in half diagonally. Cut the 3N strips into 2¾″ × 5⅜″ (7.5 cm × 13.5 cm) pieces. Cut the side-triangle squares in quarters diagonally and the corner-triangle squares in half diagonally.

2. Make the half-square triangle units for the pieced blocks and borders. Check for accuracy; each unit should measure 2⅛″ (5.5 cm).

3. Unit construction: see diagram.

4. Block sew order: see diagram.

5. Sew the pieced blocks, alternate blocks, and side and corner triangles together in a diagonal set. Trim and straighten the edges if necessary.

6. Use the remaining half-square triangle units and the dark 2⅛″ (5.5 cm) corner squares to construct the pieced borders. See page 121 for help. Attach the pieced borders and the light middle border strips to complete the quilt top.

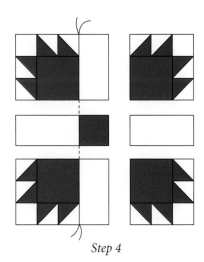

Step 4

KALEIDOSCOPE

Katie Prindle, quilted by Anna Venti

Block size: 6″ (15 cm)

Techniques: Quick-cutting or Template 4B, and Template 5A

   Note: If working in metric, use a 0.6 cm rather than a 0.75 cm seam allowance

Setting: Straight

Fabric suggestions: Variety of light fabrics for small triangles. Medium and dark fabrics for large triangles

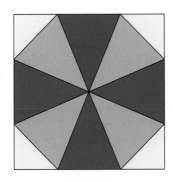

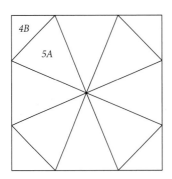

Cutting

Step 2

Step 3

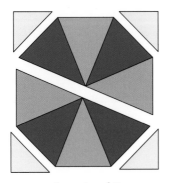

Steps 4 and 5

		Crib/Wall	Twin	Double/Queen	King
Finished size	*(inches)*	42 × 54	72 × 90	84 × 96	108 × 96
	(centimeters)	*109 × 135*	*180 × 225*	*210 × 240*	*270 × 240*
Blocks set		7 × 9	12 × 15	14 × 16	18 × 16
Total blocks		63	180	224	288

FABRIC *(Based on 42″ to 44″/106 cm to 112 cm selvage to selvage)*

		Crib/Wall	Twin	Double/Queen	King
4B: scraps to total	*(yards)*	¾	1¾	2¼	2¾
	(meters)	0.7	1.6	2.1	2.5
5A: scraps to total	*(yards)*	3	8	10	13
	(meters)	2.7	7.3	9.1	12
Backing	*(yards)*	1¾	5¼	5⅝	8½
	(meters)	1.6	4.8	5.1	7.8
Binding	*(yards)*	⅜	½	⅝	¾
	(meters)	0.3	0.5	0.6	0.7

CUTTING

		Crib/Wall	Twin	Double/Queen	King
4B: 2⅝″ (7 cm) strips		8	23	28	36
5A*: 4″ (10.3 cm) strips		26	72	90	115
Backing	*(lengths)*	1	2	2	3

* The height of Template 5A is slightly less than 4″/10.3 cm. Measure to determine the exact width for the cut strips

CONSTRUCTION

1. Cut the 4B strips into 2⅝″ (7 cm) squares, then cut in half diagonally. Use Template 5A to mark the strips and cut the angles.
2. Sew light and dark triangles together in pairs, as shown. Press seams open.
3. Join pairs of triangles to make half blocks. Press seams open. *Helpful Hint:* Lay out all the blocks before attaching corners. Turn to achieve interesting designs. Some corners are attached to light triangles.
4. Block sew order; see diagram. Press final seam open.
5. Attach the corner triangles.

THOUSAND PYRAMIDS

Diana McClun, quilted by Anna Venti

Techniques: Templates 6A, 6B, 6C, and optional quick-cutting
Fabric suggestions: Scraps for pieced units, and border fabrics to complement your quilt top

Unit 1   Unit 2

		Crib/Wall	Twin	Double/Queen	King
Finished size	*(inches)*	47 × 59	71 × 91	87 × 95	107 × 99
	(centimeters)	*119 × 150*	*180 × 231*	*221 × 241*	*272 × 251*
Horizontal rows		13	21	22	23
Units per row		37	31	39	49
Unit 1		413	559	734	963
Unit 2		68	92	124	164

FABRIC *(Based on 42″ to 44″/106 cm to 112 cm selvage to selvage)*

		Crib/Wall	Twin	Double/Queen	King
Scraps to total	*(yards)*	4	7	8½	10½
	(meters)	*3.7*	*6.4*	*7.8*	*9.6*
Inner border	*(yards)*	2	3	3¼	3¼
	(meters)	*1.8*	*2.7*	*3*	*3*
Outer border, side triangles, and binding					
	(yards)	2	3	3¼	3¼
	(meters)	*1.8*	*2.7*	*3*	*3*
Backing	*(yards)*	3¾	5⅝	9	9
	(meters)	*3.4*	*5.1*	*8.2*	*8.2*

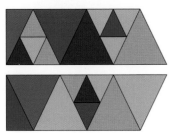

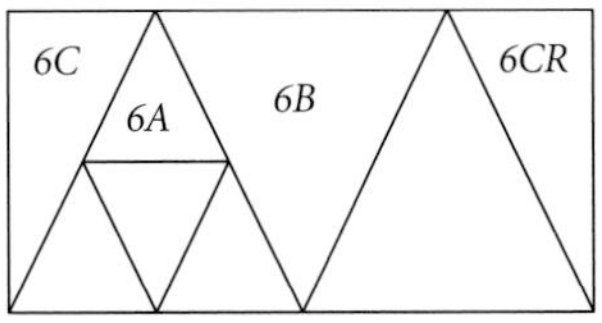

Cutting

CUTTING

		Crib/Wall	Twin	Double/Queen	King
6A: 2¾″ (7 cm) strips		3	5	6	8
6B: 4⅞″ (12.5 cm) strips		29	44	52	68
Inner border	*(inches)*	1¾	1¾	1¾	1¾
	(centimeters)	*4.5*	*4.5*	*4.5*	*4.5*
Side triangles					
6C and 6CR,*each		13	21	22	23
Outer border	*(inches)*	2½	2½	2½	2½
	(centimeters)	*6.5*	*6.5*	*6.5*	*6.5*
Backing	*(lengths)*	2	2	3	3

*R = reverse template on fabric

CONSTRUCTION

1. Use the templates to cut the angles on the 6A and 6B strips.
2. Unit 2 sew order: see diagram. Unit 2 is placed randomly throughout the quilt.
3. Sew order: see diagram.

Step 2

Step 3

HEART

Diana McClun and Laura Nownes, quilted by Kathy Sandbach

Block size: 6″ (15 cm)

Techniques: Quick-cutting or Template 1K, and appliqué (Template 4S)

Setting: Straight with sashing and posts

Fabric suggestions: A variety of fabrics for backgrounds, posts, and hearts. Two fabrics to complement the appliquéd heart blocks for borders

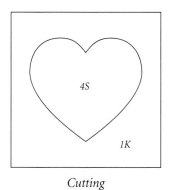

Cutting

		Crib/Wall	Twin	Double/Queen	King
Finished size	*(inches)*	42 × 58	74 × 90	82 × 90	98 × 98
	(centimeters)	*105 × 145*	*185 × 225*	*205 × 225*	*245 × 245*
Blocks set		4 × 6	8 × 10	9 × 10	11 × 11
Total blocks		24	80	90	121

FABRIC *(Based on 42″ to 44″/106 cm to 112 cm selvage to selvage)*

		Crib/Wall	Twin	Double/Queen	King
Backgrounds and posts					
Scraps to total *(yards)*		1	3¼	3½	4⅝
	(meters)	*0.9*	*3*	*3.2*	*4.2*
Hearts					
Scraps to total *(yards)*		½	1½	1¾	2¼
	(meters)	*0.5*	*1.4*	*1.6*	*2.1*
Sashing	*(yards)*	¾	2¼	2⅝	3¼
	(meters)	*0.7*	*2.1*	*2.4*	*3*
Inner border	*(yards)*	1⅜	2¼	2¼	2½
	(meters)	*1.3*	*2.1*	*2.1*	*2.3*
Outer border	*(yards)*	1¾	2⅝	2⅝	2⅞
	(meters)	*1.6*	*2.4*	*2.4*	*2.6*
Backing	*(yards)*	1⅞	5⅜	5⅜	8⅝
	(meters)	*1.7*	*4.9*	*4.9*	*7.9*
Binding	*(yards)*	⅜	½	⅝	¾
	(meters)	*0.3*	*0.5*	*0.6*	*0.7*

CUTTING

		Crib/Wall	Twin	Double/Queen	King
1K: 6½″ (16.5 cm) squares		24	80	90	121
4S: Template		24	80	90	121
Posts					
2½″ (6.5 cm) strips		3	7	7	9
Sashing					
2½″ (6.5 cm) strips		10	28	35	44
Inner border	*(inches)*	2	2	2	2
	(centimeters)	*5.3*	*5.3*	*5.3*	*5.3*
Outer border	*(inches)*	5	5	5	5
	(centimeters)	*12.8*	*12.8*	*12.8*	*12.8*
Backing	*(lengths)*	1	2	2	3

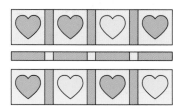

Step 3

CONSTRUCTION

1. Cut the 1K strips into 6½″ (16.5 cm) squares and the post strips into 2½″ (6.5 cm) squares. Cut the sashing strips into 2½″ × 6½″ (6.4 cm × 16.5 cm) pieces.
2. Appliqué all hearts (4S) to the background squares using one of the methods described in Chapter 6.
3. Sew the blocks together in a straight set, joining them with the sashing and posts. See page 112 for help, if needed.

POSTAGE STAMP BASKETS

Kandy Petersen

Block size: 12″ (30 cm)
Techniques: Quick-cutting or Templates 1D, 4M, and 4P, and appliqué (Template 8D)
Setting: Straight
Fabric suggestions: Light color for background and border, and a variety of colors for baskets

		Crib/Wall	Twin	Double/Queen	King
Finished size	*(inches)*	48 × 60	72 × 84	84 × 96	108 × 96
	(centimeters)	120 × 150	180 × 210	210 × 240	270 × 240
Blocks set		3 × 4	5 × 6	6 × 7	8 × 7
Total blocks		12	30	42	56

FABRIC *(Based on 42″ to 44″/106 cm to 112 cm selvage to selvage)*

		Crib/Wall	Twin	Double/Queen	King
Background, border and binding	*(yards)*	2¾	5¼	6⅝	8¼
	(meters)	2.5	4.8	6.1	7.5
Baskets **Scraps to total**	*(yards)*	1½	3¼	4¼	5½
	(meters)	1.4	3	3.9	5
Backing	*(yards)*	3½	5	5¾	8½
	(meters)	3.2	4.6	5.3	7.8

CUTTING

	Crib/Wall	Twin	Double/Queen	King
Background				
4M: 4⅞″ (12.5 cm) strips	6	15	21	28
1D: 2½″ (6.5 cm) strips	6	15	21	28
Border (cut crossgrain and pieced): 6½″ (16.5 cm) strips	5	8	9	9
Baskets				
4P: 2⅞″ (7.5 cm) squares	48	120	168	224
4M: 4⅞″ (12.5 cm) squares	48	120	168	224
Backing *(lengths)*	2	2	2	3

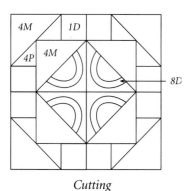

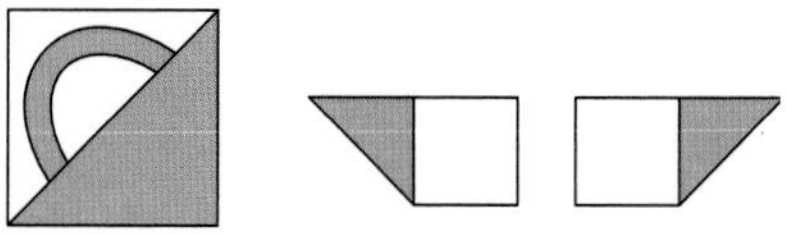

Cutting

CONSTRUCTION

1. Cut the 4M background strips into 4⅞″ (12.5 cm) squares, then cut in half diagonally. Cut the 4P squares in half diagonally. Cut the 1D strips into 2½″ (6.5 cm) squares. Cut the 4M basket squares in half diagonally (*8D = one-half of 4M basket triangles with Template 8D*).
2. Appliqué the 8D handles to the 4M background pieces using one of the methods described in Chapter 6.
3. Unit construction: see diagrams.
4. Block sew order: see diagram.
5. Sew the blocks together in a straight set.
6. Attach the borders to complete the quilt top.

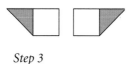

Step 3

Step 4

GINGERBREAD HOUSE

Diana McClun and Laura Nownes, quilted by Kathy Sandbach

House block size: 9″ × 12″ (22.5 cm × 30 cm)

Tree block size: 6″ × 12″ (15 cm × 30 cm)

Techniques: Quick-cutting and double half-square triangles, or Templates 1F, 1L, 2R, 3C, 3F, 3K, 3P, and 4D, and Templates 7E, 8C, and 9A

Setting: Straight

Fabric suggestions: Variety of fabrics for pieced blocks, and two fabrics to complement pieced blocks for the pieced border

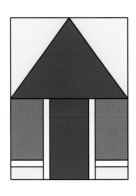

	Crib/Wall	Twin	Double/Queen	King
Finished size *(inches)*	48 × 60	66 × 84	84 × 96	102 × 96
(centimeters)	120 × 150	165 × 210	210 × 240	250 × 240
House blocks set	4×4	6×6	8×7	10×7
House blocks	16	36	56	70
Tree blocks	8	12	14	14
Gingerbread blocks	16	22	28	34

FABRIC *(Based on 42″ to 44″/106 cm to 112 cm selvage to selvage)*

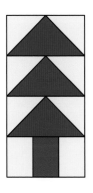

		Crib/Wall	Twin	Double/Queen	King
House blocks					
Sky					
Scraps to total	*(yards)*	¾	1¼	1¾	2¼
	(meters)	0.7	1.1	1.6	2.1
Roof					
Scraps to total	*(yards)*	¾	1¼	1½	1⅞
	(meters)	0.7	1.1	1.6	1.7
House fronts					
Scraps to total	*(yards)*	⅝	1¼	1½	1⅞
	(meters)	0.3	0.7	1.0	1.3
Door					
Scraps to total	*(yards)*	⅜	¾	1⅛	1⅜
	(meters)	0.2	0.6	0.7	1.0
House trim					
Scraps to total	*(yards)*	¼	⅝	¾	1⅛
	(meters)	0.9	2.5	3.2	3.8
Tree blocks					
Sky					
Scraps to total	*(yards)*	¾	⅞	1	1
	(meters)	0.7	0.8	1	1
Trees					
Scraps to total	*(yards)*	½	¾	¾	¾
	(meters)	0.6	0.7	0.7	0.7
Trunks					
Scraps to total	*(yards)*	⅛	⅜	½	⅝
	(meters)	0.1	0.3	0.5	0.6
Gingerbread blocks					
Scraps to total	*(yards)*	⅜	½	⅝	¾
	(meters)	0.3	0.5	0.6	0.7
Pieced border (top and bottom), two fabrics, each	*(yards)*	⅜	½	⅝	¾
	(meters)	0.3	0.5	0.6	0.7
Backing	*(yards)*	3½	5	5⅝	8½
	(meters)	3.2	4.6	5.1	7.8
Binding	*(yards)*	⅜	½	⅝	¾
	(meters)	0.3	0.5	0.6	0.7

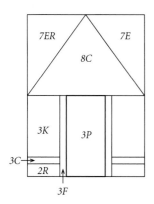

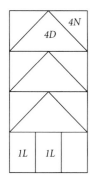

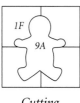

Cutting

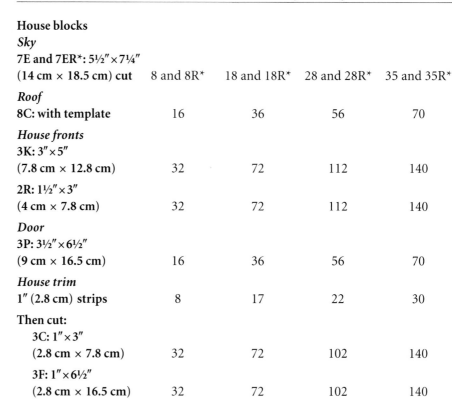

	Crib/Wall	Twin	Double/Queen	King
FABRIC *(Based on 42″ to 44″/106 cm to 112 cm selvage to selvage)*				
House blocks				
Sky				
7E and 7ER*: 5½″ × 7¼″				
(14 cm × 18.5 cm) cut	8 and 8R*	18 and 18R*	28 and 28R*	35 and 35R*
Roof				
8C: with template	16	36	56	70
House fronts				
3K: 3″ × 5″				
(7.8 cm × 12.8 cm)	32	72	112	140
2R: 1½″ × 3″				
(4 cm × 7.8 cm)	32	72	112	140
Door				
3P: 3½″ × 6½″				
(9 cm × 16.5 cm)	16	36	56	70
House trim				
1″ (2.8 cm) strips	8	17	22	30
Then cut:				
3C: 1″ × 3″				
(2.8 cm × 7.8 cm)	32	72	102	140
3F: 1″ × 6½″				
(2.8 cm × 16.5 cm)	32	72	102	140
Tree blocks				
Sky				
4N: 3½″ (9 cm) squares	6 per block	6 per block	6 per block	6 per block
1L: 2½″ × 3½″				
(6.5 cm × 9 cm)	2 per block	2 per block	2 per block	2 per block
Trees				
4D: 3½″ × 6½″				
(9 cm × 16.5 cm)	3 per block	3 per block	3 per block	3 per block
Trunks				
1L: 2½″ × 3½″				
(6.5 cm × 9 cm)	8	12	14	14
Pieced borders				
1F: 3½″ (9 cm) strips, each	3	5	5	6
Gingerbread blocks				
9A: Template	16	22	28	34
Backing *(lengths)*	2	2	2	3

*R = reverse template on fabric

Step 1

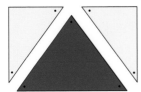

Step 2

Step 3

Step 4

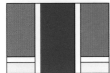

Step 5

CONSTRUCTION

1. Cut the sky 7E and 7ER pieces in half diagonally, alternating the cutting direction, as shown.
2. Sky/roof unit: see diagram. This unit can be tricky to sew accurately. Therefore the sky fabric was cut slightly too large to allow for trimming the unit to measure 9½″ × 6½″ (24 cm × 16.5 cm). *Helpful Hint:* Mark dots on the wrong sides of the fabric shapes at the seam intersections. Then match the dots on adjoining pieces.
3. House unit construction: see diagram.
4. Block sew order: see diagram.
5. Trees: use the double half-square triangle technique to make the tree units.
6. Block sew order: see diagram.
7. Pieced border: join strips in pairs, then cut every 3½″ (9 cm), as shown.
8. Unit construction: see diagram.
9. Use your preferred method of appliqué to attach the gingerbread boys. Refer to Chapter 6 for help if needed.
10. Sew the house and tree blocks together in rows. Join the rows, then attach the gingerbread border to complete the quilt top.

Note: The roofs on the quilt photographed were trimmed with wide rickrack.

Step 6

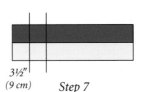

3½″
(9 cm)   *Step 7*

Step 8

PINEAPPLE LOG CABIN

Freddy Moran

Block size: 17″ (43 cm)

Techniques: Quick-cutting. This is a unique block construction therefore no template patterns are given.

Setting: Straight

Fabric suggestions: One fabric for block centers, inner border and binding, a variety of fabrics for the pieced blocks and border units and one fabric to complement the pieced blocks for the setting triangles in the border

		Crib/Wall	Twin	Double/Queen	King
Finished size	(inches)	47 × 47	64 × 81	81 × 81	98 × 98
	(centimeters)	119 × 119	163 × 206	206 × 206	249 × 249
Blocks set		2 × 2	3 × 4	4 × 4	5 × 5
Total blocks		4	12	16	25
Total pieced border units		32	54	60	76

FABRIC *(Based on 42″ to 44″/106 cm to 112 cm selvage to selvage)*

		Crib/Wall	Twin	Double/Queen	King
Centers, inner border and binding	(yards)	1	1¼	1½	1½
	(meters)	0.9	1.1	1.4	1.4
Pieced blocks and border units, Light and dark scraps to total	(yards)	2	6	10	12
	(meters)	1.8	5.5	9.1	11
Setting triangles	(yards)	1	1½	1¾	2
	(meters)	0.9	1.4	1.6	1.8
Backing	(yards)	3	5	5	8⅝
	(meters)	2.7	4.6	4.6	7.9

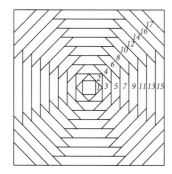

CUTTING

		Crib/Wall	Twin	Double/Queen	King
Pieced blocks **Centers: 2″ (5.1 cm)** squares		4	12	16	25
Strips	(inches)	1⅝	1⅝	1⅝	1⅝
	(centimeters)	4	4	4	4
Corners: 4″ (10.2 cm) squares, dark		8	24	32	50
Pieced border units **2⅝″ (6.7 cm) strips**		9	15	15	21
Setting triangles **Sides: 7″ (17.8 cm) strips**		3	5	6	7
Ends: 4″ (10 cm) squares		8	8	8	8
Border	(inches)	2	2	2	2
	(centimeters)	5.3	5.3	5.3	5.3
Backing	(lengths)	2	2	2	3

Step 2

Step 3

CONSTRUCTION

1. Cut the 4″ (10 cm) corner squares for the blocks in half diagonally. Cut the 2⅝″ (6.7 cm) strips for the pieced border units for the blocks into 2⅝″ (6.7 cm) squares. Then cut the squares in half diagonally. For the border setting triangles: cut the 7″ (17.8 cm) strips into 7″ (17.8 cm) squares, then cut the squares in quarters diagonally for the sides; cut the 4″ (10 cm) squares in half diagonally for the ends.

2. Accurately mark diagonal lines in both directions on each 2″ (5.5 cm) center square, as shown.

3. Sew four different light strips around the center square, as shown. Trim and straighten the edges. The unit should measure 4¼″ (10.5 cm). To keep blocks symmetrical, check that the distances from the marked center lines to each side measure 2⅛″ (5.25 cm)

4. Place the unit on the cutting board, as shown. Position your ruler over the unit with the 1¼″ (3.5 cm) markings directly over the diagonal lines on the center square. Make the first cut beyond the edges of the ruler on both the top and right sides.

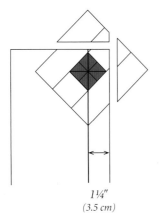

1¼″
(3.5 cm)

Step 4

5. Rotate the unit. Again, place the 1¼″ (3.5 cm) markings on the ruler directly over the diagonal lines on the center square. Make the second cut beyond the edges of the ruler on both the top and right sides, as shown.

6. Sew four different dark fabrics around the unit. Trim the excess lengths and square the unit to measure 3½″ (9.5 cm).

7. Place the unit on the cutting board. Position your ruler over the unit with the 1¾″ (4.7 cm) markings directly over the vertical lines on the center square. Make the first cut beyond the edges of the ruler on both the top and right sides, as shown.

8. Rotate the unit and repeat the cutting for the remaining two sides. The 1¾″ (4.7 cm) markings will be in line with the vertical lines on the center square. The 3½″ (9.5 cm) markings will be in line with the bottom and left sides.

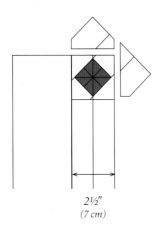

2½″
(7 cm)

Step 5

Note: All remaining rows are assembled and cut in the same manner, alternating the addition of light and dark strips around the unit. The measurement for placement on the diagonal or vertical lines of the center block will increase by ½″ (1.25 cm) with each new addition. The outside measurement (after the first rotation) will increase by 1″ (2.5 cm). Beginning with Row 5 the unit will have eight sides instead of four, as shown.

Step 6

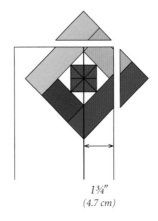

1¾″
(4.7 cm)

Step 7

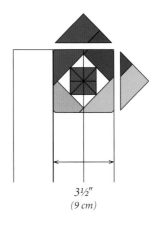

3½″
(9 cm)

Step 8

As the unit increases in size it will no longer be possible to line up the markings on your ruler with the outside edges after the first rotation. Be very careful with cutting as you will only be able to use the markings on the center square for positioning. Check to see that the unit remains square after each new addition and cut.

The following chart will be a quick reference for measurements.

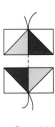

Step 12

Row	Strips	First cut	Second cut
1	Light	1¼″ (3.5 cm)	2½″ (7 cm)
2	Dark	1¾″ (4.7 cm)	3½″ (9.5 cm)
3	Light	2¼″ (6 cm)	4½″ (12 cm)
4	Dark	2¾″ (7.2 cm)	5½″ (14.5 cm)
5	Light	3¼″ (8.5 cm)	6½″ (17 cm)
6	Dark	3¾″ (9.7 cm)	7½″ (19.5 cm)
7	Light	4¼″ (11 cm)	8½″ (22 cm)
8	Dark	4¾″ (12.2 cm)	9½″ (24.5 cm)
9	Light	5¼″ (13.5 cm)	10½″ (27 cm)
10	Dark	5¾″ (14.7 cm)	11½″ (29.5 cm)
11	Light	6¼″ (16 cm)	12½″ (32 cm)
12	Dark	6¾″ (17.2 cm)	13½″ (34.5 cm)
13	Light	7¼″ (18.5 cm)	14½″ (37 cm)
14	Dark	7¾″ (19.7 cm)	15½″ (39.5 cm)
15	Light	8¼″ (21 cm)	16½″ (42 cm)
16	Dark	8¾″ (22.2 cm)	17½″ (44.5 cm)
17	Dark	8¾″ (22.2 cm)	17½″ (44.5 cm)

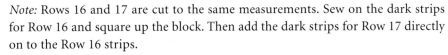

Note: Rows 16 and 17 are cut to the same measurements. Sew on the dark strips for Row 16 and square up the block. Then add the dark strips for Row 17 directly on to the Row 16 strips.

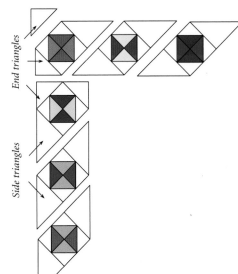

Step 13

9. Add the corner triangles to complete the block.

10. Sew the blocks together in a straight set.

11. Attach the inner border.

12. Make the half-square triangles for the pieced border. Then join four together to make units, as shown.

13. Join the units with the setting triangles, referring to the sew order diagram. Trim and straighten the edges.

14. Attach the pieced borders to complete the quilt top.

BLOSSOMING TREE

Diana McClun and Laura Nownes, quilted by Kathy Sandbach

Block size: 12″ (30 cm)
Techniques: Quick-cutting, strip piecing, and half-square triangles or Templates 1B, 1D, 4M, and 4P
Setting: Diagonal
Fabric suggestions: One fabric for background, another for tree trunk, scraps for tree, three fabrics for pieced sashing, fabric for setting triangles to complement your pieced blocks

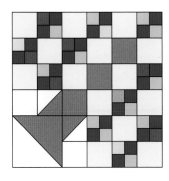

	Crib/Wall	Twin	Double/Queen	King
Finished size *(inches)*	47 × 47	68 × 90	90 × 90	110 × 90
(centimeters)	*116 × 116*	*168 × 221*	*221 × 221*	*273 × 221*
Blocks set	2 × 2	3 × 4	4 × 4	5 × 4
Total blocks	5	18	25	32

FABRIC *(Based on 42″ to 44″/106 cm to 112 cm selvage to selvage)*

		Crib/Wall	Twin	Double/Queen	King
Background	*(yards)*	½	¾	1	1
	(meters)	*0.5*	*0.7*	*0.9*	*0.9*
Tree blocks					
Trunk	*(yards)*	⅜	1¼	1¼	1¾
	(meters)	*0.3*	*1.1*	*1.1*	*1.6*
Tree					
Scraps to total					
	(yards)	¾	2½	3	4¼
	(meters)	*0.7*	*2.3*	*2.7*	*3.9*
Pieced sashing, each of					
three fabrics	*(yards)*	⅜	¾	1	1¼
	(meters)	*0.3*	*0.7*	*0.9*	*1.1*
Posts	*(yards)*	⅛	⅜	½	⅝
	(meters)	*0.1*	*0.3*	*0.5*	*0.6*
Side and corner					
triangles	*(yards)*	¾	2⅛	2⅛	2¾
	(meters)	*0.7*	*1.9*	*1.9*	*2.5*
Backing	*(yards)*	3	5¼	8	8
	(meters)	*2.7*	*4.8*	*7.3*	*7.3*
Binding	*(yards)*	⅜	½	⅝	¾
	(meters)	*0.3*	*0.5*	*0.6*	*0.7*

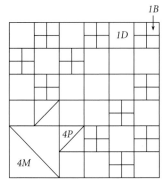

CUTTING

	Crib/Wall	Twin	Double/Queen	King
Background				
1D: 2½″ (6.5 cm) strips	1	3	4	4
4P: 2⅞″ (7.5 cm) strips	1	2	2	2
4M: 4⅞″ (12.5 cm) strips	1	2	2	2
Trunks				
1D: 2½″ (6.5 cm) strips	1	4	5	6
4P: 2⅞″ (7.5 cm) strips	1	2	2	3
4M: 4⅞″ (12.5 cm) strips	1	4	4	6
Tree				
1B: 1½″ (4 cm) strips	8	30	40	52
1D: 2½″ (6.5 cm) strips	5	16	22	28
Pieced sashing				

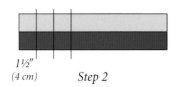

1½″
(4 cm)

Step 2

Step 3

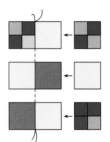

Make two per block

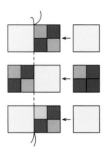

Make one per block

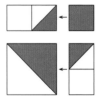

Make one per block

Step 5

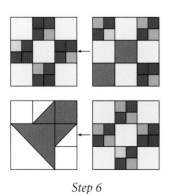

Step 6

1½″ (4 cm) strips, each fabric 6	16	22	27
Posts			
3½″ (9 cm) strips	1	3	4	5
Side triangles			
24″ (61 cm) squares	1	3	3	4
Corner triangles			
14″ (36 cm) squares	2	2	2	2
Backing *(lengths)*	2	2	3	

CONSTRUCTION

1. Cut all 1D strips into 2½″ (6.5 cm) squares. Cut all 4P strips into 2⅞″ (7.5 cm) squares, then cut in half diagonally. Cut all 4M strips into 4⅞″ (12.5 cm) squares, then cut in half diagonally. Cut the post strips into 3½″ (9 cm) squares. Cut the side-triangle squares in quarters diagonally and the corner-triangle squares in half diagonally.

2. Make several combinations of 1B strips, then cut the sets every 1½″ (4 cm), as shown.

3. Unit construction: see diagram.

4. Make half-square triangle units from background and trunk fabrics.

5. Unit construction: see diagrams.

6. Block sew order: see diagram. Refer to the photograph for exact color placement.

7. For the sashing, sew three sashing fabric strips together in sets. Cut every 12½″ (31.5 cm), as shown.

8. Join the blocks, sashing strips, posts, and side and corner triangles in a diagonal setting, as shown.

9. Trim and straighten the edges to complete the quilt top.

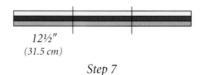

12½″
(31.5 cm)

Step 7

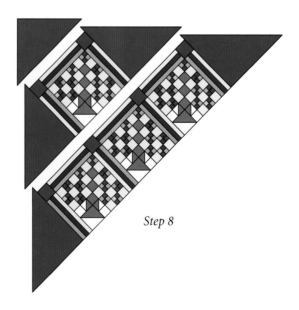

Step 8

DRUNKARD'S PATH

Maker unknown, c. 1910–1930

Block size: 6″ (15 cm)
Techniques: Templates 3Q, 3R, and 4H, and optional quick-cutting
Setting: Straight
Fabric suggestions: Four colors of your choice

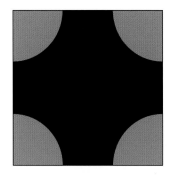

Block 1

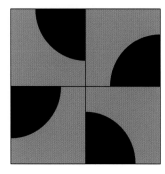

Block 2

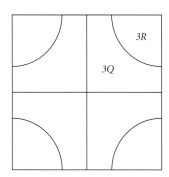

Cutting

	Crib/Wall	Twin	Double/Queen	King
Finished size *(inches)*	37 × 49	61 × 73	85 × 97	109 × 97
(centimeters)	*98 × 128*	*158 × 188*	*218 × 248*	*278 × 248*
Blocks set	3 × 5	7 × 9	11 × 13	15 × 13
Block 1	8	32	72	98
Block 2	7	31	71	97

FABRIC *(Based on 42″ to 44″/106 cm to 112 cm selvage to selvage)*

	Crib/Wall	Twin	Double/Queen	King
Color #1 (black), borders				
and binding *(yards)*	2¾	4⅝	6⅜	7½
(meters)	*2.5*	*4.2*	*5.8*	*6.9*
Color #2 (salmon) *(yards)*	¾	1¼	3	4
(meters)	*0.7*	*1.1*	*2.7*	*3.7*
Color #3 (blue) *(yards)*	¾	1⅛	1½	1⅝
(meters)	*0.7*	*1*	*1.4*	*1.5*
Color #4 (brown) *(yards)*	¾	1⅛	1⅝	1¾
(meters)	*0.7*	*1*	*1.5*	*1.6*
Backing *(yards)*	3⅜	4¾	9	9
(meters)	*3.1*	*4.3*	*8.2*	*8.2*

CUTTING

	Crib/Wall	Twin	Double/Queen	King
Color #1 (cut lengthwise)				
Inner border, *(inches)*	2	2	2	2
(centimeters)	*5.3*	*5.3*	*5.3*	*5.3*
Outer border				
(inches)	2	2	2	2
(centimeters)	*5.3*	*5.3*	*5.3*	*5.3*
4H: 5½″ (14 cm) strips	4	6	8	9
3Q: 3½″ (9 cm) strips	3	11	24	33
3R: 2½″ (7.8 cm) strips	2	8	18	25
Color #2				
3Q: 3½″ (9 cm) strips	3	11	24	33
3R: 2½″ (7.8 cm) strips	2	8	18	25
Color #3				
3Q: 3½″ (9 cm) strips	6	10	13	15
Color #4				
3R: 2½″ (7.8 cm)strips	4	7	10	12
Backing *(lengths)*	2	2	3	3

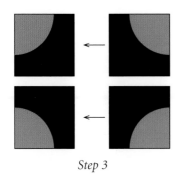

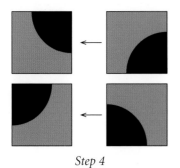

Step 3

CONSTRUCTION

1. Cut the 4H strips into 5½″ (14 cm) squares, then cut in quarters diagonally. Cut the 3Q strips into 3½″ (9 cm) squares. Then use Template 3Q to mark and cut the curves. Cut the 3R strips into 2½″ (6.5 cm) squares. Then use Template 3R to mark and cut the curve.

2. Sew the 3Q and 3R pieces together to make units.

3. Block 1 sew order: see diagram.

4. Block 2 sew order: see diagram.

5. Attach the inner border.

6. Assembly: alternate Blocks 1 and 2, starting with Block 1 in the corner.

7. Pieced border sew order: see diagram.

Helpful Hint: See the Drunkard's Path Practice Exercise in Chapter 5 for help.

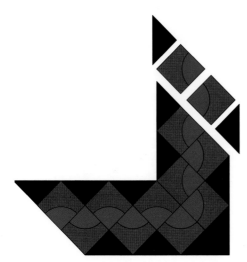

Step 4

Step 5

STAR OF BETHLEHEM

Diana McClun and Laura Nownes, quilted by Kristina Volker

Techniques: Quick-cutting, strip piecing, and double half-square triangles or Templates: crib/wall, 1B, 1D, 4K, 4R, 6F; twin, 1E, 2N, 4C, 4G, 6E; double/queen and king, 1E, 2N, 4C, 4G, 6D

Fabric suggestions: Six fabrics for stars and pieced border, one light fabric for background

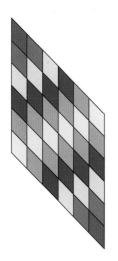

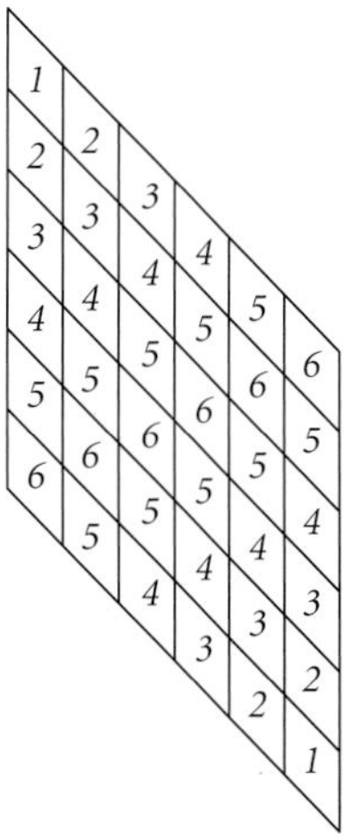

		Crib/Wall	Twin	Double/Queen
Finished size *(inches)*		52 × 52	68 × 68	85 × 85
(centimeters)		*135 × 135*	*174 × 174*	*218 × 218*

FABRIC *(Based on 42″ to 44″/106 cm to 112 cm selvage to selvage)*

		Crib/Wall	Twin	Double/Queen
Color #1	*(yards)*	⅜	½	⅝
	(meters)	*0.3*	*0.5*	*0.6*
Color #2	*(yards)*	½	⅝	¾
	(meters)	*0.5*	*0.6*	*0.7*
Color #3	*(yards)*	⅝	¾	1
	(meters)	*0.6*	*0.7*	*0.9*
Color #4	*(yards)*	¾	⅞	1⅛
	(meters)	*0.7*	*0.8*	*1*
Color #5	*(yards)*	⅞	1	1⅜
	(meters)	*0.8*	*0.9*	*1.3*
Color #6	*(yards)*	⅝	¾	1
	(meters)	*0.6*	*0.7*	*0.9*
Background	*(yards)*	1¾	2¾	4¼
	(meters)	*1.6*	*2.5*	*3.9*
Inner border	*(yards)*	⅝	1¾	2¼
	(meters)	*0.6*	*1.6*	*2*
Backing	*(yards)*	3	4½	7½
	(meters)	*2.7*	*4.1*	*6.9*
Binding	*(yards)*	⅜	½	⅝
	(meters)	*0.3*	*0.5*	*0.6*

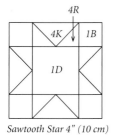

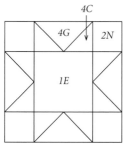

4R

4K | 1B

1D

Sawtooth Star 4″ (10 cm)

4C

4G | 2N

1E

Sawtooth Star 5″ (12 cm)

Cutting

CUTTING

Center star		Crib/Wall	Twin	Double/Queen
Strip width *(inches)*		2	2½	3
(centimeters)		5	6.5	8
Color #1		2	2	2
Color #2		4	4	4
Color #3		6	6	6
Color #4		8	8	8
Color #5		10	10	10
Color #6		6	6	6
Background				
Side triangles, one square *(inches)*		21 × 21	27 × 27	34 × 34
(centimeters)		*58 × 58*	*70 × 70*	*87 × 87*
Corner squares, each *(inches)*		15 × 15	20 × 20	24 × 24
(centimeters)		*38 × 38*	*50 × 50*	*60 × 60*
Inside border *(inches)*		1½	1¼	2
(centimeters)		*4*	*3.2*	*5.3*

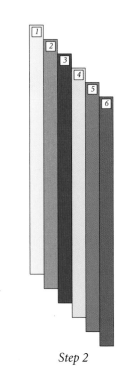

Step 2

	Crib/Wall	Twin	Double/Queen
Star border			
Strips	7	7	11
1B or 2N, width *(inches)*	1½	1¾	1¾
(centimeters)	4	4.5	4.5
Strips	4	4	6
4K or 4G, width *(inches)*	2½	3	3
(centimeters)	6.5	7.5	7.5
Strips	4	4	6
4R or 4C, width *(inches)*	1½	1¾	1¾
(centimeters)	4	4.5	4.5
Strips	2	2	3
1D or 1E, width *(inches)*	2½	3	3
(centimeters)	6.5	7.5	7.5
Alternate blocks	24	24	32
(inches)	4½ × 4½	5½ × 6	5½ × 5½
(centimeters)	11.5 × 11.5	13.5 × 15	13.5 × 13.5
Backing *(lengths)*	2	2	3

CONSTRUCTION

1. Cut the square for the side triangles into quarters diagonally. Cut the 1B/2N and the 4R/4C strips into 1½" (4 cm) or 1¾" (4.5 cm) squares, depending on the size of your strips (see cutting chart). Cut the 4K/4G strips into 1½" × 2½" (4 cm × 6.5 cm) pieces for the crib/wall quilt or 1¾" × 3" (4.5 cm × 7.5 cm) pieces for other quilt sizes. Cut the 1D/1E strips into 2½" (6.5 cm) or 3" (7.5 cm) squares depending on the size of your strips (see cutting chart).

2. Sew two sets of each of the following color combinations, offsetting the strips exactly as shown in the diagram. Press all seams in each set toward the first strip.

     1–2–3–4–5–6   2–3–4–5–6–5   3–4–5–6–5–4

   Helpful Hint: Apply spray sizing to stabilize the sets.

3. Turn the set as shown, then use the 45° angle on your wide plastic ruler to measure and cut diagonal strips 2" (5 cm), 2½" (6.5 cm), or 3" (8 cm) wide, depending on the size of your quilt. *Warning:* This is a critical step, as these angles can be hard to achieve. Be as accurate as possible, and don't rush. You may have to readjust the cut edge after two or three strips.

4. Block sew order for main quilt: see diagrams.

5. Assembly: The technique required to construct this pattern by machine is called "Y-seam construction." You *must not* stitch into the seam allowance at the crook of the Y. Stitch in the direction of the arrows in the diagram. The distance from A to B must be the same on each corner and triangle piece. Measure and pin for accuracy before sewing. Press the seams between the assembled diamond units open. *Note:* This is one of the few instances in quilt-making in which seams are pressed open rather than to one side. Open seams eliminate bulk and allow the diamond points to join accurately at the center of the star.

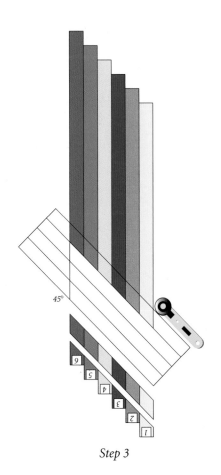

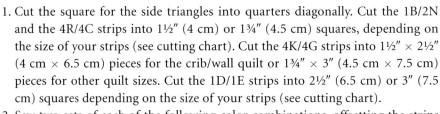

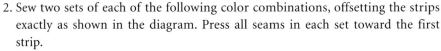

Step 3

Step 4

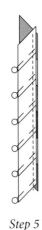

Step 5

6. The background corner squares and side triangles are cut slightly too large. Straighten the edges and trim the excess fabric as necessary to allow first the inner border then the pieced border to fit properly. *Note:* Star sizes vary, you may have more space between the star points and the inner border than that shown in the sample quilt.

7. Make the pieced border stars. For the crib/wall quilt, make 24 stars (4″/10 cm); for the twin, make 24 stars (5″/12 cm); and for the double/queen, make 32 stars (5″/12 cm). Join the star blocks to the alternate border blocks to make the pieced border. *Helpful Hint:* See page 41 for help with construction.

8. Attach the inner border and then the pieced border to complete the quilt top.

Step 7

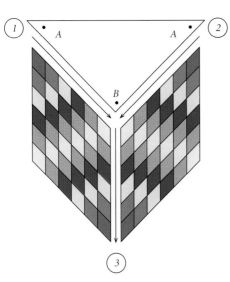

Step 6

ALL STARS SAMPLER

Dafri Estes, quilted by Kathy Sandbach

Block size: 12″ (30 cm)
Techniques: Quick-cutting, strip piecing, half-square triangles, double half-square triangles, and templates
Setting: Straight with vertical and horizontal sashing; one size only
Fabric suggestions: Scraps for pieced blocks, fabric to complement for sashing and border

		Twin/Wall
Finished size	*(inches)*	$52\frac{1}{2} \times 89$
	(centimeters)	*131 × 223*

FABRIC *(Based on 42″ to 44″/106 cm to 112 cm selvage to selvage)*

Sashing,* two fabrics each	*(yards)*	$2\frac{1}{2}$
	(meters)	*2.3*
Outer border	*(yards)*	$2\frac{1}{2}$
	(meters)	*2.3*
Inner border	*(yards)*	$2\frac{1}{4}$
	(meters)	*2*
Pieced blocks, scraps to total	*(yards)*	5
	(meters)	*4.6*
Backing	*(yards)*	$5\frac{1}{2}$
	(meters)	*5*

* *Includes corner blocks, horizontal and vertical sashing, and binding*

CUTTING AND CONSTRUCTION

Sashing, blue	*(inches)*	$2\frac{1}{2}$
	(centimeters)	*6.5*
Sashing, yellow	*(inches)*	2
	(centimeters)	*5.3*
Inside border	*(inches)*	$3\frac{3}{4}$
	(centimeters)	*9.8*
Horizontal sashing	*(inches)*	$1\frac{1}{2}$
	(centimeters)	*4*
Inner corner blocks, four each	*(inches)*	$2\frac{1}{2} \times 2\frac{1}{2}$
	(centimeters)	*6.5 × 6.5*
Outer border	*(inches)*	$4\frac{1}{2}$
	(centimeters)	*11.5*
Outer corner blocks, four each	*(inches)*	$4\frac{1}{2} \times 4\frac{1}{2}$
	(centimeters)	*11.5 × 11.5*
Backing	*(lengths)*	2

Memory (make two)

1. Cut the following for each block:
   4P: Eight 2⅞″ (7.5 cm) squares, four each of two fabrics
   Sixteen 2½″ (6.5 cm) squares, eight each of two fabrics
   4F: Eight 2½″ × 4½″ (6.5 cm × 11.5 cm) pieces, four each of two fabrics
   1D: Eight 2½″ (6.5 cm) squares
   1H: One 4½″ (11.5 cm) square
2. Cut the 4P 2⅞″ (7.5 cm) squares in half diagonally.
3. Make half-square triangle and double half-square triangle units, as shown.
4. Unit construction: see diagrams.
5. Block sew order: see diagram.

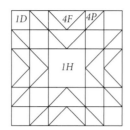

Make two combinations

Step 3

Step 4

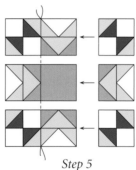

Step 5

54-40 or Fight (make two)

1. Cut the following for each block:
   1D: Twenty 2½″ (6.5 cm) squares
   8A: Four with template
   8AR*: Eight with template
   8B: Four with template
2. Unit construction: see diagram.
   Helpful Hint: Mark dots on the wrong sides of shapes 8A, 8AR, and 8B at the intersection of seam allowances for ease in matching and sewing.
3. Block sew order: see diagram.

*R = reverse template on fabric

Step 2

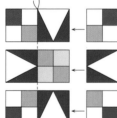

Step 3

Swamp Angel (make two)

1. Cut the following for each block:
   4M: Four 4⅞″ (12.5 cm) squares, two each of two fabrics
   1H: One 4½″ (11.5 cm) square
   4F: Four 5¼″ (13.6 cm) squares
2. Cut the 4M squares in half diagonally and the 4F squares in quarters diagonally.
3. Unit construction: see diagrams.
4. Block sew order: see diagram.

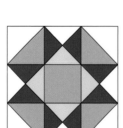

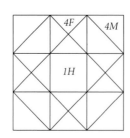

Make four *Make four*

Step 3

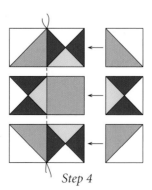

Step 4

Square and Stars *(make two)*

1. Cut the following for each block:
   2S: Four 2⅝″ (6.8 cm) squares
   2U: One 4¾″ (12.1 cm) square
   4N: Two 3⅞″ (10 cm) squares
   1F: Four 3½″ (9 cm) squares
   4J: Six 4¼″ (11.1 cm) squares
2. Cut the 4N squares in half diagonally and the 4J squares in quarters diagonally.
3. Unit construction: see diagrams.
4. Block sew order: see diagram.

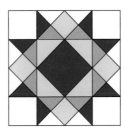

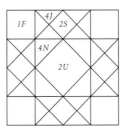

Make one   *Make four*

Step 3

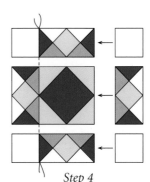

Step 4

Variable Star *(make two)*

1. Cut the following for each block:
   1H: Five 4½″ (11.5 cm) squares
   4F: Four 5¼″ (13.6 cm) squares
2. Cut the 4F squares in quarters diagonally.
3. Block sew order: see diagram.

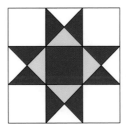

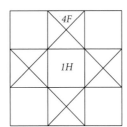

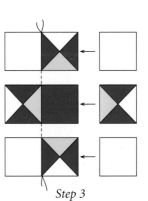

Step 3

Le Moyne Star *(make two)*

1. Cut the following for each block:
   1G: Four 4″ (10.3 cm) squares
   4E: One 6¼″ (16.1 cm) square
   6D: Eight with template
2. Cut the 4E squares in quarters diagonally.
3. The technique required to construct the block by machine is called "Y-seam construction." You must not stitch into the seam allowance at the crook of the Y.
   Helpful Hint: Indicate the stopping points with dots on the templates and the wrong side of each appropriate fabric piece as indicated in the diagram. Stitch in the direction indicated by the arrows. Press seams joining diamonds open.
4. Unit construction: see diagram.
5. Block sew order: see diagram.

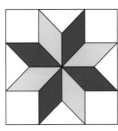

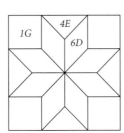

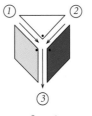

Step 3

Make four

Step 4

Step 5

Chapter 2

COLOR SELECTION

 Color is magic in quilts. More than pattern or design, it is the single element that tells us most about the quilt— and the person who made it. We are all aware of the importance and power of color. However, many of us are insecure about our color choices when we project from fabric swatches to an entire quilt. We want the color to fall into place, to make us feel excited and creative. We want the quilt to enhance the environment for which it was intended. We want the choices to say "ME!"

Because of the overwhelming abundance of fabrics available, the selection of color is an extremely difficult task. Do not let any negative thoughts you may have with regard to your ability to choose the "right" colors get in the way of your starting on a quilt—today! We are giving you solid guidelines for choosing a color scheme. Use them to give yourself confidence in developing your own individual style. If you are a beginner, think of this as your "first" quilt and not your "one and only." The important step now is to begin. Trust yourself.

COLOR SCHEMES

MONOCHROMATIC

As the name implies, only one color is used in this scheme. All the shades, tints, and tones that can be made from that color are considered. Just think of all the different greens there are in nature and you can produce a monochromatic color scheme. Take a pair of scissors and go out into your garden or yard. Clip a variety of greenery from the various plants and grasses. Take these clippings back into the house and lay them out on a white (or light neutral) surface. Study the clippings and you will soon

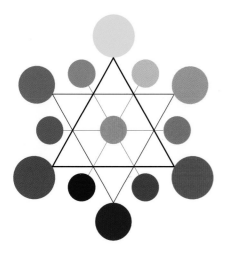

be excited by the variety of tints and tones. If your choice is a monochromatic color scheme, this simple exercise can be your guide when you go to buy your fabric. Diana used this exercise to plan her *Thousand Pyramids* quilt on page 58.

ANALOGOUS

This scheme is made by referring to the color wheel and selecting adjacent colors. These colors just naturally go together because they share a color in common. For example, in the use of violet, blue-violet, and blue, you can expand the scheme by adding blue-green and green and, for more variety, include the five colors that have blue in common.

COMPLEMENTARY

This scheme uses one color and its complement—red and green, blue and orange, yellow and violet. Opposite colors tend to give brilliance and purity to each other. Together, they attract attention. See Patti's red and green sampler quilt on page 145.

PRIMARY

This scheme predominantly uses the primary colors—red, yellow, and blue. The primary colors are spaced at equal distance around the color wheel, so an equilateral triangle can be drawn to connect them. This color scheme is always successful, because you have a warm color (red), a cool color (blue), and a light color (yellow) to give good contrast and sparkle. This color scheme is never dull. See Diana and Laura's *Roman Square* quilt on page 14.

Another triadic (three) color scheme is orange, violet, and green. These will also create a lively combination. If orange, violet, and green sounds displeasing as a combination, try using peach, lavender, and light green.

RAINBOW

This color scheme uses all twelve colors from the color wheel and sequences them in their natural order as in a spectrum. We associate rainbows with happiness and a fresh new start. See Diana's *Attic Windows* quilt on page 42.

WARM AND COOL

The color wheel shows the fairly even distribution of warmth and coolness. Most people give more attention to the warm colors because of their dynamic qualities. The warm colors are: red, red-orange, orange (rust and brown), orange-yellow, and yellow. These are the colors of the earth and sand. The cool colors are blue, blue-green, violet, and their combinations. These are the colors of the sky, water, and night. The cool colors have the optical effect of receding in space, so a blue block would seem farther away than a brown one. The warm colors seem closer and larger in size. This is important to the image you want to create. The warm colors also unify shapes and forms placed on them. The cooler colors seem to separate the shapes into more independent units. This gives a crisp, sharp effect. If you want to suggest perspective, combine the warm colors with the receding cool colors. See Dale Fleming's second quilt block on page 91.

LIGHT AND DARK

The use of only two colors produces sharp contrast, and the shape and design elements are highly visible. There is no clutter, and the simplicity of the color scheme is always very attractive. See the *Bear's Paw* quilt on page 53.

NEUTRAL

Neutrals are mostly naturals: earth, wood, sand, ice, shells, pebbles, straw, bone, ivory, pine cones, wicker, reed. They also represent manmade materials such as concrete, metal, and glass. These colors are particularly important to a quilter, because they age with grace. Dirt, fading, and aging do not ruin their looks; in fact, they can become enhanced. They are peaceful to view and live with; they do not offend us. They will enhance other colors, so they make marvelous backgrounds. They are classic, dramatic, and always correct.

SCRAP BAG

Choose every and any group of colors from your scrap bag. You can close your eyes, shake a paper bag full of scraps, and just pick out twelve or more pieces. Now spread out the scraps and select a single color—preferably one that is missing or an appealing one among the scraps—to unify the parts of the quilt, as in Log Cabin with its traditionally red center squares. See Diana and Laura's *Log Cabin* on page 18, Katie Prindle's *Kaleidoscope* on page 56, and *Spool* on page 44.

TRADITIONAL

In traditional color schemes there is a dominant color, a subordinate color, and an accent color. As a rule, you choose a moderately bland color as a dominant one, a slightly brighter color for the secondary support, and a much brighter color in small amounts for accent. See Laura's *Pine Tree* quilt on page 50.

DEVELOPING A COLOR SCHEME

In choosing a color scheme, you need to start with some idea of what you want your color combination to achieve. The overall mood you want your quilt to have might be soft, romantic, bold, dramatic, or sophisticated. Your starting point can be your favorite fabric, a decorative item in your bedroom, a wall or floor covering, a picture from a book or magazine, or an object from nature. An item can help you establish a mood, then a color combination. It is through the analysis of colors in your object, by looking and seeing, that you can be assured your combination will produce the effect you wish to carry over into your quilt.

Selection of fabric for a color scheme takes time, and it is difficult to know which colors should be used and which discarded, but this choice makes the selection YOU. This personal choice is the basis of individual work, and who has the right to say it is lively, good, mediocre, or poor? Yes, only YOU.

PRACTICE EXERCISE: Creating a Color Scheme

This Practice Exercise involves observing an object of your choice from which to choose a color scheme. Choose something whose colors you find exciting, like a painting, a flower, or a seashell. Write down on a piece of paper exactly what you see.

1. Describe the shape and line (straight lines, curves, sharp angles, etc.)

2. List the colors you see and give a description (light pink, dark blue, dull green, soft yellow, etc.).

3. How much of each color is there?

4. Is there a background color?

5. Look in depth: upside-down, around, underneath, within. Next, assimilate your observations and translate them into fabrics. Consider not only your object's color(s), but also its form, texture, and pattern; do not ignore the interplay of these ingredients.

This method of developing a color scheme has worked with success in our basic quilting classes. Once you have selected your fabrics, you can concentrate and enjoy the quiltmaking process rather than worry about the colors; you will be confident that they will work well together. Very often, novices making a quilt will become bored with their fabric selections and yearn to add something new. For this reason, we suggest that you allow yourself a fairly wide variety of fabrics.

Coloring a *Memory* Block

To help you develop your own color sense, we asked four quiltmakers with individualistic styles to share their methods of developing color schemes. Each quilter was given a line drawing of the block pattern *Memory* and asked to develop a color scheme. Because color selection is both important and personal, you will want to study how others use, see, and evaluate their choices, but don't be afraid to use your imagination. Be original!

Barbara Engleking

My first instinct for this block was to use my favorite color combination—red and green. I also wanted to use my favorite fabric—large florals from Hoffman's Coventry line. As a shop owner, I always try to convince people to do two things when selecting fabric: Vary the value, and vary the scale. I also try to persuade them to use prints rather than limiting themselves to so many tone-on-tone (solid) fabrics. *Memory* is a great block to play with for value practice, because there are many different parts that can be emphasized to change the entire appearance. For example, by making different value choices, you can lose the stars completely, or you can emphasize the one created where the blocks join.

LaVonne J. Horner

As a quilter, I enjoy combining fabrics in unusual ways, so the possibility of using eight fabrics for this block was very appealing to me. I especially enjoy the challenge of incorporating batiks into my work. The key for me is to use strong colors. Here, the block design recedes, with the use of a strong color in the corners, and becomes secondary to the design that occurs where the blocks meet. I enjoy fooling the eye this way.

Angie Dawson Woolman

The abundant choices of available fabric are wonderful—and often overwhelming. Every time I begin selecting fabrics, I first imagine what I want as the value contrast between the block pattern pieces. Next, I pick a palette of fabrics that reflects my value needs and my color/print interests. This stage is both agonizing and intriguing because I like to consider fabrics that expand my previous comfort zone. For this *Memory* block, I wanted to work with warm and cool color contrasts and fabrics with strong prints. My palette began with five or six fabrics, and, as I positioned various choices, I added some and replaced others. I also considered the secondary effects of putting my four *Memory* blocks together.

Dale Fleming

In my quilts, I like to play with color and motion. The first thing one sees in this block is the central star, so I decided to put the emphasis there. I cut out squares of a full range of colors and arranged them on a felt pattern board in a pattern I liked. This quilt has a background of cool colors (green to magenta) with an "S" of warm colors (yellow to red) running through it. The central square was too big for me, so I put a lighter value of each color in the center of each star. That left a light, medium, and dark for each color and gave a feeling of depth. At this point, everything was just floating and nothing felt connected. I wanted a strong line out of the black squares to give a feeling of continuity between the stars and squares. After playing with many fabrics and the pieces in the diamond, I decided that expanding circles worked well. Unfortunately, the black squares were now too black, so I put in two other values. The black between the yellow and the lime is much lighter than the one between the purple and the navy.

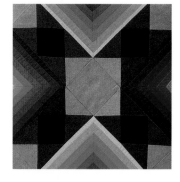

Dale Fleming

In this version of *Memory,* I tried a very different approach. I decided to use the entire color wheel. I put cool colors (purple to green) at the top, warm colors (yellow to red) in the center, and then cool colors again at the bottom. This makes the top and bottom recede, while the center of the block comes forward. When looking at the block, a secondary pattern of diamonds kept peeking through, so I decided to let them really stand out. Each diamond either comes forward (dark on the outside, light in the center) or recedes (light on the outside, dark in the center). I wanted the star part of the block to remain in the background. I accomplished that with three values of black that give the illusion of overlapping squares or a plaid. In the finished block, by emphasizing different shapes, several patterns emerge, giving the quilt a three-dimensional feel.

A CHECKLIST FOR CHOOSING FABRIC

Now that you have made your color selection, here is a helpful checklist for making your purchases:

1. Is the fabric 100% cotton?

2. Are there any one-way designs (stripes, plaids, etc.)? If so, be sure to purchase extra yardage—⅝ yard (60 cm) minimum—to allow for cutting.

3. Do you have enough variety in color, design, and scale? Try to avoid fabrics that are all the same type of design (florals, etc.).

4. Have you chosen a good "ground" fabric? This is the fabric (or fabrics) that will be used as the background of the individual blocks. It is best to use a solid fabric or one that will "read" as a plain fabric, such as a small overall print.

5. Do the fabrics have an overall appeal? Do you not only *like* the combination, but *love* it? If so, congratulate yourself. This was a big decision, and now you are ready to make your purchases.

After shopping, take your fabric home. Relax. Your next job will be to prepare the fabric for cutting.

Chapter 3

FABRIC PREPARATION

 There are three approaches to fabric preparation and the beginning quilter should be aware that this is a subject of much debate. Read through these descriptions; then, make a choice. Whichever you choose, test your fabrics for colorfastness before proceeding to cut and sew.

WAYS TO PREPARE FABRIC

PRE-SHRINKING YOUR FABRIC

Quilters need their fabrics to shrink *before* (not after) the quilt is made.

1. Separate your lights from darks for washing.

2. Unfold fabric to a *single thickness*. If you do not and the fabric is not colorfast, you may end up with splotchy fabric.

3. Place the fabric in warm (*not* hot), clear water. *Do not* use detergent. Allow the fabric to absorb the water thoroughly.

4. Look to see if the fabric is bleeding color into the water. If it is, follow Steps 4 to 6 in "How to Determine If Your Fabric Is Colorfast" below.

5. If the fabric is colorfast, remove it from the water and tumble dry it in your dryer until it is slightly damp. Iron.

PRE-WASHING YOUR FABRIC

This approach not only pre-shrinks the fabric but makes it safer to use.

1. Follow Steps 1 and 2 above.

2. Place the fabric in warm (*not* hot) water with detergent (or a detergent substitute). Using detergent will reduce chemical irritants and allergens, but washing also removes chemicals that resist mildew and bacteria.

Washed cotton will also lose some of its "body;" it will be softer.

3. Rinse your fabric *at least* four times in clear water. Dry.

4. Check to see if your washed fabric is colorfast. If it is, iron. If it is not, follow Step 6 in "How to Determine If Your Fabric Is Colorfast."

WORKING WITH "NEW" FABRIC

Many quilters like the look and feel of "new" fabrics. They make quilts without pre-shrinking or pre-washing the fabrics, and report no problems. Be aware that your fabric (when it is eventually washed) will shrink *at least* 1½% to 3%. However, it will be more soil resistant and less likely to mildew if left unwashed. Test your fabrics for colorfastness. *Warning:* If you do not, a fabric may bleed into another when you wash your quilt.

IS YOUR FABRIC COLORFAST?

1. Cut a small triangle of each fabric.

2. Immerse one of these swatches into a clear glass of warm water.

3. Check to see if there is any color change in the water. If it remains clear, then you can proceed. Test the remaining swatches, one at a time.

4. In each case, if the water has changed color, then remove the excess dye by washing the entire piece of fabric in the washing machine (one or two washings) in clear, warm water—*no detergent or soap.*

5. Cut another triangle of the washed fabric and re-test it in a clear glass of warm water. If there is no color change, proceed to "Straightening Your Fabric."

6. If the water still changes color, you will have to set the dye. To do so, immerse the fabric into a full-strength solution of white vinegar. *Do not dilute it with water.* The amount of vinegar required will depend upon the size of the fabric, approximately 1 gallon (4 liters) of white vinegar for 3 yards (meters). Rinse it thoroughly two to three times in clear, warm water. Re-test in a clear glass of warm water. If there is no color change, dry the fabric completely, iron it, and proceed to straighten it. If there is a color change, *do not* use the fabric in your quilt.

Very few fabrics will require this much attention. The ones to be watchful for are the deep red tones, teals and purples.

STRAIGHTENING YOUR FABRIC

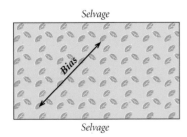

Selvage

Bias

Selvage

Often the fabric you have purchased is not straight. You can straighten it by pulling gently along the bias. Some quilters find it easier to straighten their fabric after it has been washed or shrunk.

You are now ready to move on to Chapter 4 and begin cutting.

Chapter 4

CUTTING

 With knowledge of the techniques in this and the following chapters, you will be able to make every quilt in this book. Read through them step by step, taking time to practice until you feel comfortable enough to start making your quilt.

General instructions for many quick and traditional methods are given and marked accordingly. Read through them; then, if you are a novice, do the Practice Exercises that follow and decide which methods you feel most comfortable with. You may decide to combine traditional methods with quick methods; many quiltmakers do. The Practice Exercises give detailed instructions for beginners. Although the general instructions will be sufficient for many experienced quiltmakers, any needleworker can benefit from completing the Practice Exercises, which are filled with useful information.

CUTTING YOUR FABRIC

Cotton fabric varies in width. For purposes of this book, the width of the fabric is assumed to be 42″ to 44″ (106 cm to 112 cm) selvage to selvage. Unless otherwise instructed, fabric strips are cut on the crosswise grain (selvage to selvage).

QUICK-CUTTING—NONDIRECTIONAL FABRIC

1. Place your fabric on your cutting board. Fold it in half lengthwise with the right side of the fabric facing you and the selvage edges even with each other. Then fold the fabric in half again, lengthwise, bringing

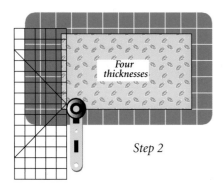

Step 2

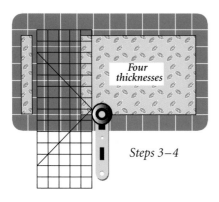

Steps 3–4

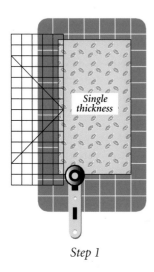

Step 1

the folded edge even with the selvage edges. There are now four thicknesses.

2. Place the wide plastic ruler perpendicular to the folded edge. If you have a cutting board marked with lines, you can skip this step and line up the fabric with the lines on your board.

3. Make a cut along the right edge of the ruler with the rotary cutter. Hold the cutter straight, not with the blade turned out, otherwise the cut edge will not be straight. Placing the weight of your free hand on the ruler, *push the cutter away from you with one strong motion, placing pressure on the board and keeping the blade tight against the ruler.* This will give a smoothly cut edge. *Do not make short, jerky cuts.*

4. Slide the ruler over to the right, so that the marking for the desired strip width on your ruler is even with the cut edge of the fabric. Run the rotary cutter along the right edge of the ruler, cutting off a strip of fabric. Unfold the strip and check to see that it is straight. *Helpful Hint:* If there is a bend in the strip where the fabric was folded, you will need to refold it; chances are that your selvage edges were not even to begin with.

QUICK-CUTTING—DIRECTIONAL FABRIC

These fabrics will give the best results if cut on the lengthwise grain. You will cut through only one thickness at a time, following the printed pattern, as you will not be able to see if underlying layers are being cut straight along the pattern. It is advised that you purchase no less than ⅝ (60 cm) yard if you are using a directional print. This will give you 22½″ (60 cm) along the lengthwise grain.

1. Lay out a single thickness of fabric on your cutting board, with the right side facing up. Using the rotary cutter and wide plastic ruler, cut off the selvage edge.

2. In order to cut an accurate width of fabric, place the desired strip width marking of your ruler even with the cut edge of the fabric.

3. Run your rotary cutter along the edge of the ruler, cutting off a strip of fabric.

4. Continue cutting strips along the lengthwise grain the required width for the pattern you have selected. Be careful to keep the printed pattern straight when cutting. *Warning:* If you are using ⅝ yard (60 cm) of fabric and the pattern has instructed you to cut four 2″ (5 cm) strips, you will need to double that (eight strips), as your strips will only be 22½″ (60 cm) long rather than the 44″ (112 cm) strips you cut from the nondirectional fabrics.

CUTTING SHAPES FROM STRIPS

Other shapes used in pieced quilt block patterns can be cut from strips, as shown on the next page.

TRADITIONAL CUTTING—NONDIRECTIONAL FABRIC

1. Lay the fabric out on a flat surface. Fold it in half lengthwise with the *wrong* side facing you and the selvage edges even with each other. Then fold the fabric in half again, lengthwise, bringing the folded edge even with the selvage edges. There are now four thicknesses.

2. Because the left-hand edge may not be straight, use your wide plastic ruler and lead pencil (white, gray, or silver for dark fabrics) to draw a line perpendicular to the folded edge and just inside the left-hand edge. Then, measuring from this line, mark the required width of the strip for the pattern you have selected. Place pins between the marked lines to hold your fabric layers in place. Using your fabric scissors, cut the strip apart on the marked lines, cutting through all four thicknesses. *Helpful Hint:* When you are cutting multiple layers, keep your scissors perpendicular to the fabric to ensure a straight cut of all layers.

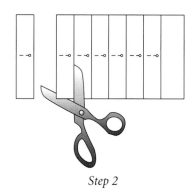

Step 2

TRADITIONAL CUTTING—DIRECTIONAL FABRIC

This method is exactly the same as the quick method, except that you use your scissors rather than a rotary cutter.

CUTTING FABRIC USING TEMPLATES

1. With the wrong side facing up, place a single thickness of fabric on your cutting board.

2. Arrange the templates on the fabric, the grainline on the templates corresponding to the lengthwise grain of the fabric.

3. Using a sharp lead, white, gray, or silver pencil, trace around each template.

4. Fold the fabric up to four thicknesses with the marked portion on top. Secure with pins inside the marked lines to hold the layers in place. Cut the fabric pieces apart using your fabric scissors, taking long, even strokes, or use the rotary cutter, wide plastic ruler, and cutting board to cut on all the marked lines.

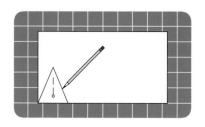

Step 4

Squares

Half-square triangles

Rectangles

Quarter-square triangles

Cutting shapes from strips

Chapter 5

PIECING

In Chapter 1 you saw the many quilts that can be made using this book. In this chapter we give the techniques necessary to make them. Once you begin making the quilt of your choice from Chapter 1, the directions for completing that quilt will refer you back here for more specific instructions on techniques.

Quilts can be made using traditional methods of quiltmaking or with "quick" methods. Traditional methods involve making a pattern (called a template) for each individual part of the quilt block. Template patterns for all the blocks (except *Pineapple Log Cabin*) included in this book are given on pages 160 to 168. The template patterns can be used for both hand and machine piecing. You can trace your own templates from them. This will save you the time of having to draft (make an outline of the individual parts on graph paper) your own pattern. We do, however, feel that some knowledge of drafting is important, so lessons on drafting have been included in Chapter 11. Take the time to do the drafting Practice Exercises. They will give you confidence in drafting patterns not included in this book or, possibly, designing a quilt block of your own.

HAND PIECING

Hand piecing gives a soft edge to the seams and, with small, even running stitches in rhythmic motion, allows the quilter who enjoys hand work to produce beautiful hand-pieced quilts. This method gives more accuracy and control than machine piecing, allowing you to make precise curved seams (see the *Drunkard's Path* quilt on page 75, the Practice Exercise on the next page, and some of the more complex pieced patterns. Because you never stitch into the seam allowance, you can turn any seam allowance in any direction; you therefore have more freedom in the sew order.

SEWING THE PIECES

Mark ¼″ (0.75 cm) stitching lines on the wrong side of every fabric piece using a small C-thru ruler and pencil.

In hand piecing, the running stitch is preferred for sewing the fabric pieces together. Stack three to five stitches on your needle at one time.

1. To thread your needle (#10 Betweens), cut approximately 18″ (45 cm) of cotton thread diagonally—the resulting sharper end will enter the eye easily. Use a single strand of thread without a knot. *Helpful Hint:* The eye of the Betweens needle is small and can be difficult to thread. A needle threader may be useful.

2. Place the two pieces of fabric to be sewn right sides together and use pins placed at right angles to the sewing line to secure. The stitching line is ¼″ (0.75 cm) from the cut edges of the pieces. Place pins at the beginning and ending points to avoid any possible shifting.

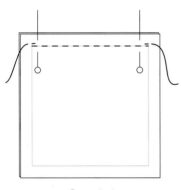

Steps 2–3

3. Starting at the beginning of the marked line, take two small backstitches, leaving a 1″ (3 cm) tail. Then continue across the line with small running stitches. Keep the tension even, neither too tight nor too loose. When you reach the end of the marked line take two backstitches. Cut the thread, leaving a 1″ (3 cm) tail. *Do not make knots.*

This hand piecing gives great control over fitting shapes together so they match perfectly at the junctions. *Never stitch into the seam allowances;* when adding new shapes, stitch only on the line. Then, when needed, flip back the seam allowance and continue sewing. Check often to see that the marked line on the front piece is lined up with the marked line on the back piece. Sew the pieces together in units.

PRACTICE EXERCISE: Making a 12″ (30 cm) *Drunkard's Path* Block

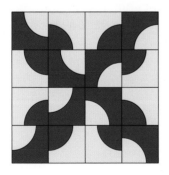

For help with making templates, see page 111

1. Lay your template plastic over Templates 3Q and 3R (see page 161) and secure with drafting tape.

2. Use the permanent pen and small C-Thru ruler to trace accurately around the outside of the two template patterns.

3. Remove the tape and plastic.

4. Use your paper scissors to cut out the two plastic templates carefully, just inside the marked lines.

5. Use your permanent pen to mark the following on each template:
  Block: *Drunkard's Path*
  Template: 3Q or 3R
  Block size: 12″ (30 cm)
  Direction of lengthwise grain and center mark on curves

6. Cut from each fabric: eight 2½″ (6.5 cm) squares and eight 3½″ (9 cm) squares. Then use Template 3R to mark and cut the curves on the 2½″ (6.5 cm) squares, and use Template 3Q to mark and cut the curves

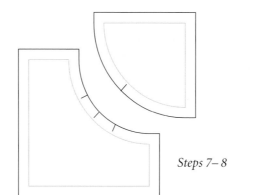

Steps 7–8

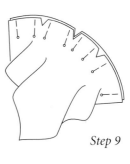

Step 9

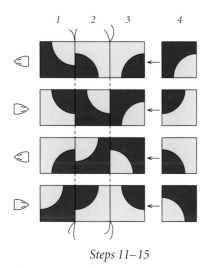

Steps 11–15

on the 3½″ (9 cm) squares.

7. Use your small C-Thru ruler to mark the stitching lines and the center of the curves on each fabric piece. Stitching lines are indicated with dotted lines on the template patterns.

8. Use the small scissors to make clips—stopping ¹⁄₁₆″ (0.15 cm) from the stitching line—at the center of the curves on all fabric pieces.

9. With right sides of the fabrics together, lay a 3Q piece on top of a 3R piece of the opposite color, matching up the center clips. Place sequin pins at the clips to hold the pieces in place. Also line up the two pieces on the straight seam lines and place pins to hold them securely. Place two more pins along the curved edges to keep them even for stitching.

10. Use hand-piecing techniques to sew the units together.

11. Lay the units out *exactly* as shown in the diagram.

12. Sew the four units in Row 1 together with the four units in Row 2, with a chain of thread joining the units, as shown.

13. Sew the four units in Row 3 to those in Row 2, chaining between units.

14. Repeat for Rows 3 and 4.

15. Alternately press the seams in the directions indicated by the arrows in the diagram.

16. Place two rows with right sides together. Pin at the seam intersections so the seams will remain turned in opposite directions. Sew the two rows together.

17. Attach additional rows in the same manner.

18. Press the seams between the rows on the wrong side, then the right side.

19. Your block is complete and should measure 12½″ (31.5 cm) square.

MACHINE PIECING OR STRIP PIECING

The easiest patterns contained in this book are made up only of strips *(Roman Square, Fence Rail,* and *Nine-Patch)*. The width of the strip is determined by the particular pattern (see Chapter 1). The technique required to make these blocks is called "strip piecing." Following the general instructions, a Practice Exercise for making a 12″ (30 cm) *Fence Rail* block is given. The exercise will guide you through the cutting and sewing of the strips, help you feel comfortable with the cutting techniques you learned in Chapter 4, and give you confidence to move on to some of the more difficult patterns involving squares and triangles.

THINGS TO KNOW ABOUT YOUR SEWING MACHINE BEFORE YOU BEGIN

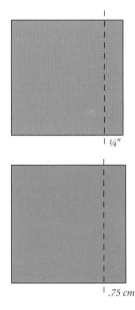

¼″

.75 cm

In quiltmaking, all sewing is done with ¼″ (0.75 cm) seam allowance. The seam allowance is the distance from the cut edge of the fabric to the line of stitching. *Unless otherwise indicated, we will be using ¼″ (0.75 cm) seam allowances throughout this book.*

If you are planning to sew your quilt on the sewing machine, it will be necessary to make an accurate ¼″ (0.75 cm) seam on the machine. To determine this distance, place your large C-Thru ruler under the presser foot and measure ¼″ (0.75 cm) to the right. Run a piece of masking tape along this point on the throat plate. *Helpful Hint:* Several thicknesses of tape will prevent your fabric from going beyond that point. On many machines, this ¼″ (0.75 cm) is the distance from the needle to the right edge of the presser foot. Also, some machines have adjustable needle positions, allowing you to obtain an accurate ¼″ (0.75 cm) seam allowance. If this is the case for your machine, you can simply use the edge of your presser foot as a guide.

Standard throat plates have large holes designed to accommodate needle movement for decorative stitches. When doing small piecework for quilts, fabric can be pushed by the needle into this hole, causing the machine to jam. *Helpful Hint:* If you experience this problem, help is available in the form of a straight-stitch throat plate which has a smaller hole. This can be purchased from your sewing-machine dealer.

SEWING STRIPS TOGETHER

1. Set the stitch length indicator on your machine to 8 to 10 stitches per inch (3 to 4 stitches per cm). This is mark 2.5 on some models. Thread your machine on the top and the bobbin with a cotton, not quilting, thread in a color to blend with your fabrics. A neutral is always good. *It is important to use the same type of thread in both the top and the bobbin to give the best stitches.*

2. Lay out the strips you have made in the required sequence. Sew two strips right sides together along one of the 44″ (112 cm) sides. Be very careful not to pull or stretch the strips while sewing. This may cause them to become wavy. Sew on any remaining strips in the proper sequence. *Helpful Hint:* Alternate sewing direction when joining multiple strips to avoid bowing.

PRESSING YOUR PIECED STRIPS

Keep your iron and pressing surface close at hand. Use a well-padded pressing surface, an ironing board, or any level surface. A light-colored

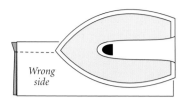

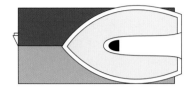

towel makes especially good padding because it keeps any seam allowance from creating a ridge on the right side of your pieced fabrics. Get in the habit of pressing often while you sew, as good pressing habits can determine the success or failure of construction. This is especially true of machine-pieced blocks. Pressing is important because it maintains flat, smooth blocks and sharp seams. We make a distinction between pressing and ironing. Pressing is an up-and-down motion, whereas ironing involves pushing the iron, which may distort the block size and stretch the pieces out of shape.

Use a steam iron with the heat control set for cotton. The steam setting will apply a little moisture to the fabric and help eliminate any wrinkles. Keep the surface of the iron smooth and clean to avoid soiling the blocks.

After you have sewn a seam, press the fabrics flat on the wrong side to set the stitches in place. Fold the top piece of fabric back, over the stitching line. Press. Seams pressed to one side are stronger than open seams. *Helpful Hint:* If darker fabrics are on top, seams will automatically be turned in the direction of the darker fabric and will not shadow through under the lighter fabric. Make your pressed seams as sharp as possible.

CUTTING YOUR PIECED STRIPS

Quick-Cutting

With the right side of the fabric facing up, lay the pressed strips on the cutting board. Using the wide plastic ruler and rotary cutter, cut the strips at the width indicated by your quilt pattern. After a few cuttings you may need to realign your cut edge with the ruler and board.

Traditional Cutting

Using a lead pencil (white, gray, or silver for dark fabrics), mark the desired width on your strips. Using your fabric scissors, cut the strips apart on the marked lines.

With just the above knowledge, a novice can begin quiltmaking. If you are new to quiltmaking, do the following Practice Exercise.

PRACTICE EXERCISE: Making a 12″ (30 cm) *Fence Rail* Block

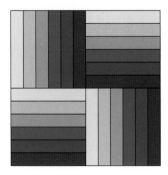

1. Using either a rotary cutter or scissors, cut one 1½″ × 44″ (3.8 cm × 112 cm) strip from each of six fabrics.

2. Lay out the strips you have made, in sequence, lightest to darkest. With the lightest strip beneath, place the next one on top of it, right sides together. Sew them together along one of the 44″ (112 cm) sides. Sew on the remaining strips in the proper sequence, working from light to dark.

3. Press the set of strips. The set should measure 6½″ (16.5 cm) wide; if it does not, check to see that each of your seam allowances is an accurate ¼″ (0.75 cm).

4. Using either the quick or traditional method of cutting pieced strips, cut the set of strips apart every 6½″ (16.5 cm). Cut four 6½″ (16.5 cm) lengths.

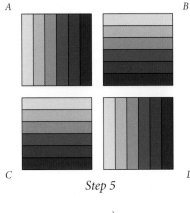

A   B

C   D

Step 5

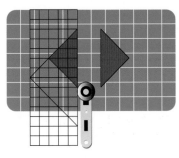

Steps 6–8

5. Lay out the four sets of strips (called units) *exactly* as shown in the diagram.

6. Pick up the top pair of units. Place B on top of A, with right sides together.

7. Stitch the two units together along the right edge, making sure the edges are aligned. Hold the two ends together while sewing.

8. Stitch the next pair of units together as in Step 7. This method of sewing units one after another without breaking the thread is called "chaining." It is helpful in keeping the units together and in the proper order during construction and it speeds up the sewing process during piecing.

9. Remove the units from the machine. Notice that the units are held together with the chain of thread. Lay one pair of units on top of the other pair, right sides together. To avoid bulky seams, finger press—that is, push the seams that come together in the center of the near-complete block in opposite directions. Secure with a pin.

10. Stitch the two pairs of units together.

11. With the block folded in half, wrong side out, press this seam. Fold the top half of the block back, over the stitching line. Press.

12. You have successfully completed your first quilt block. It should measure 12½" (31.5 cm) square. If not, double-check to see that all strips have been cut accurately; all seam allowances are an accurate ¼" (0.75 cm); and all seams are pressed sharply.

MAKING HALF-SQUARE TRIANGLES

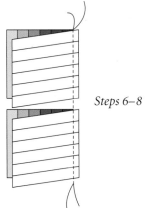

Step 2

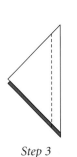

Step 3

Some quilt patterns include what is referred to as "half-square triangles." These are made up of two triangles from different fabrics sewn together along their longest sides, then pressed, to form a square. There are many time-saving methods of making these units, such as paper piecing, grids, and bias strips. The following is our preferred method.

1. Cut strips of fabric to the width indicated in the cutting charts for the pattern you are making. The width of the strips is ⅞" (2.5 cm) larger than the finished size of the unit. ("Finished" means after the unit is sewn into the quilt block.) For example, strips for a 2" (5 cm) finished unit are cut 2⅞" (7.5 cm) wide.

2. Cut the strips into squares, then cut the squares in half diagonally, as shown. *Helpful Hint:* Position the squares on the cutting board exactly as shown to ensure accurate cuts from corner to corner.

3. Place two triangles with right sides together and stitch them along their longest sides, as shown.

4. Stitch another pair of triangles directly after the first pair, as shown, without cutting the thread. *Helpful Hint:* Be consistent in stitching the lighter triangles on top for ease in pressing later.

5. Continue this method of chaining with the remaining triangles.

6. Lay the units with the darker sides facing up on the pressing board,

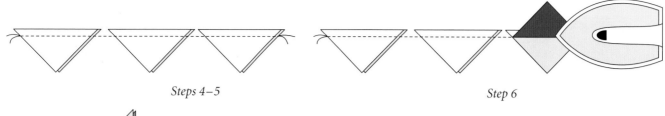

Steps 4–5   *Step 6*

Step 8

and press first on the wrong sides to set the stitches. Fold and press the darker triangles over the stitching line to form a square, as shown.

7. Cut the chain of thread attaching the units.

8. Trim the extensions and check the accuracy of the unit size. Trim and straighten the edges if necessary.

PRACTICE EXERCISE: Making a 12″ (30 cm) *Pinwheel* Block

1. Place the two fabrics with right sides together and press. Fold the fabrics to four thicknesses.

2. Use the rotary cutter to clean off the left-hand edges (right-hand edges if you are left-handed).

3. Cut one 3⅞″ (10 cm) wide strip, then cut the strip into 3⅞″ (10 cm) squares (you will need eight squares of each fabric).

4. With the squares still layered in four thicknesses and right sides together, cut them in half diagonally.

5. Make four units, as shown. *Helpful Hint:* Seams can be pressed *open* to eliminate the bulk created where the eight seams meet at the center.

6. Position the four units exactly as shown. Stitch them together to complete the block.

7. Join four of the larger units made in Step 6 to complete the block.

8. Press the completed block on the wrong side, then the right side. It should measure 12½″ (31.5) cm.

Step 4

Step 6

Step 5

MAKING DOUBLE HALF-SQUARE TRIANGLES

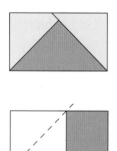

Step 1

There are several methods for sewing these three triangles together, but we like this one, because it does not involve cutting any triangles, only squares and rectangles. It is also easier for the beginner to keep the finished unit straight, especially when working with smaller blocks. Each pattern in Chapter 1 that requires them will instruct you as to the cut size of the squares and rectangles. For purposes of these directions, no specific measurements will be used.

1. With the right sides of the fabrics together, place one square piece on top of the rectangular piece. Stitch through both thicknesses diagonally across the square, as shown. Be very careful to stitch from point to point in order to keep the angle sharp. *Helpful Hint:* If you have diffi-

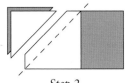

Step 2

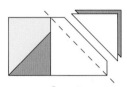

Step 3

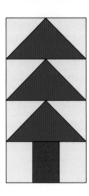

Step 4

culty sewing straight across the diagonal of the square, you can lightly press the square in half diagonally and then stitch along the fold, or lightly mark the diagonal with a pencil and then stitch along the marked line.

2. Using your rotary cutter, trim the excess fabric to within ¼″ (0.75 cm) of the stitching line.

3. Fold the resulting triangle over the stitching line and press. Take another square and place it on top of this unit as shown, then stitch across it diagonally.

4. Trim off the excess fabric to within ¼″ (0.75 cm) of the stitching line. Then proceed to fold and press as in Step 3. This completes the double half-square triangle unit.

To apply this quick technique to patterns that do not appear in this book, you must know the *finished* size of one unit. If you are unsure, draft the quilt pattern on graph paper and measure the length and width of one of its double half-square triangle units.

For the small triangles, cut squares the *finished* width of one unit *plus* ½″ (1.5 cm). For the large triangle, cut a rectangle the *finished* width of the unit *plus* ½″ (1.5 cm) × the *finished* length of the unit *plus* ½″ (1.5 cm).

PRACTICE EXERCISE: Making a 6″ × 12″ (15 cm × 30 cm) *Tree* Block

1. Cut the background fabric into six 3½″ (9 cm) squares and two 3½″ × 6½″ (9 cm × 16.5 cm) pieces. Cut the tree fabric into three 2½″ × 4½″ (6.4 cm × 11.4 cm) pieces. Cut the trunk fabric into one 1½″ × 6½″ (4 cm × 16.5 cm) piece.

2. Make three double half-square triangle units using the six background squares and three tree fabrics, as shown. Refer to the general instructions for help, if needed.

3. Stitch the background/trunk row, as shown.

4. Stitch the units together to complete the block, as shown.

5. Press the completed block on the wrong side, then the right side. It should measure 6½″ × 12½″ (16.5 cm × 31.5 cm).

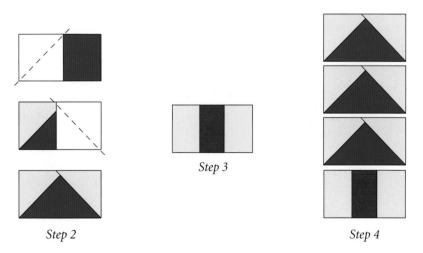

Step 2

Step 3

Step 4

Chapter 6

APPLIQUÉ

 Appliqué is as much a part of quiltmaking as is piecing. With it, designs are made by cutting pieces of one fabric and *applying* them to the surface of another. You can do much more than just take a single design and stitch it to a background fabric: you can create intricate designs by combining several elements. These methods allow you to make simple, elaborate, or complex designs such as flowers, birds, animals, figures, hearts, or symbols. You have the option of making stylized or realistic designs because of the precision in making stems, curves, points, and Vs. This method allows you to:

1. Reproduce intricate shapes accurately from a line drawing
2. Duplicate shapes exactly
3. Place shapes flat on the background fabric
4. Handle very small shapes easily
5. Make smooth, even curves and sharp points and Vs

PREPARING FOR APPLIQUÉ

PREPARING THE PATTERN

1. Trace or make a photocopy of the entire pattern.

2. Trace the required number of shapes for the overall design onto a piece of plain paper, plastic-coated freezer paper, or fusible web material (5 circles or 12 leaves, for example). Leave spaces between the shapes for easier cutting. Do not trace any stems: They will be made from bias strips of fabric. *Helpful Hint:* Use a plastic circle template to make accurate circles. Mark the grainline on each shape.

3. Use your paper scissors to cut out all of the individual shapes. Since

the shape you cut will be the shape you get, take time to cut accurately. *Helpful Hint:* If any shape in the pattern you have chosen (such as a leaf) has long, thin points, redraw the shape to have broader points. It will look just as good and will be easier to handle.

PREPARING AND MARKING THE BACKGROUND FABRIC

1. Press the fabric you plan to use as a background.

2. Cut out the background fabric, keeping the grainline straight and allowing a ¼″ (0.75 cm) seam allowance on all sides. A 12″ (30 cm) finished block would be cut to 12½″ (31.5 cm).

3. Turn the background fabric to the wrong side and, with a lead pencil, write the word "Top" and indicate the direction of the lengthwise grain in the seam allowance at the top of the block.

4. With the right side of the background fabric facing up, center it on top of the overall traced or photocopied design. Hold it in place with drafting tape. Using a #2.5 lead pencil, lightly trace 1/16″ (0.2 cm) inside each shape. In addition, stems are marked with a single line through the middle. *Helpful Hint:* When tracing a pattern onto fabric, tape the pattern to a daylight window and tape the piece of fabric over it. Then use a lead pencil to lightly trace around the pattern. Another option is to make your own light table. Use a glass table or place a piece of Plexiglas over a dining table which has been opened for insertion of its extension leaves. Place a lamp underneath the glass or Plexiglas. Place the pattern on the glass or Plexiglas and the fabric over the pattern. Lightly trace onto the fabric. This method works especially well when tracing onto dark fabrics.

PREPARING STEMS

Stems are made from bias strips of fabric. This method of preparation utilizes bias bars or ¼″ (0.75 cm) flat metal strips.

1. Cut a bias strip of fabric ⅞″ (2.5 cm) wide by 25″ (64 cm) long. This can be made from ½ yard (0.5 m) of fabric.

2. Fold the bias strip in half lengthwise with the right side facing out.

3. Machine stitch along the lengths with an accurate ⅛″ (0.4 cm) seam allowance. This will create a tube.

4. Insert the metal strip into the fabric tube and place the seam line in the center of a flat side of the bar.

5. With the metal strip still inserted in the fabric, steam press on both sides. The seam allowance is pressed to one side.

6. Remove the metal strip.

7. The stem is ready to be stitched onto the background fabric.

Step 5

PINNING AND BASTING
PAPER PATTERNS TO FABRIC

1. With the grainline marking facing you, lay the individual paper patterns on the wrong side of the fabric, leaving at least ½″ (1.5 cm) between shapes. The grainline marking on the paper pattern must correspond to the lengthwise grain of the fabric.

2. Pin the paper pattern in place with sequin pins. For freezer-paper patterns, use a dry iron to press the shapes to the fabric. For fusible web material, follow the manufacturer's instructions for bonding the material to your fabric.

3. Using small scissors, cut out the fabric around the shape, leaving an extra ¼″ (0.75 cm) cm all around the paper pattern.

4. Baste the paper pattern to the fabric and remove the pins. *Note:* This step is not required for freezer-paper patterns or fusible web material.

5. This step involves basting the seam allowance down to the wrong side of the paper pattern. Preparation for basting varies from shape to shape. Specific instructions follow. *Note:* Basting is not required for fusible web material. Follow the manufacturer's instructions for bonding the shape to the background fabric.

BASTING LEAVES

Use this method for basting leaves and other shapes with points, such as hearts.

1. Thread your needle with a single strand of thread and make a knot in one end. With the paper pattern facing you, fold the seam allowance toward you.

2. Starting on a curved side of the shape (not at its point), bring the needle up from the right side (so the knot is on the right side). Take small running stitches to hold the seam allowance in place.

3. Stitch right up to the point, then fold the seam allowance from the opposite side of the shape beyond the point and continue stitching. When you look at the right side of the shape, there should be an excess piece of fabric extending out beyond the point. This will be tucked under when the shape is sewn to the background fabric. *Do not cut it off.*

4. Press on the wrong, then the right, side.

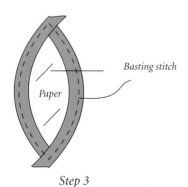

Paper
Basting stitch

Step 3

BASTING CIRCLES

1. Thread your needle with a single strand of thread and place a knot in one end. With the paper pattern facing you, take small running stitches ⅛″ (0.3 cm) away from the edge of the paper pattern, drawing up the thread as you sew. This will distribute the fullness evenly. Continue all the way around the circle. This row of stitching will not be removed.

2. Baste again around the edge of the circle through all layers to hold the seam allowance flat.

3. Press on the wrong, then the right, side.

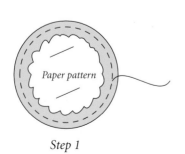

Paper pattern

Step 1

BASTING SCALLOPS

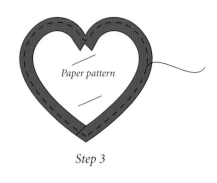

Paper pattern

Step 3

Use this method for basting scallops and shapes with Vs, such as hearts.

1. At each V make a small, straight clip into the seam allowance, stopping ¹⁄₁₆″ (0.2 cm) from the edge of the paper pattern.

2. With the paper side up, fold the seam allowance toward you. Thread your needle with a single strand of thread and place a knot in one end. Bring the needle up from the right side (so the knot is on the right side). Folding the clipped edges of the Vs out sideways to form an inverted V, take small running stitches to hold the seam allowance in place.

3. Continue around the shape. Cut the thread at the end, leaving a 1″ (3 cm) tail.

4. Press on the wrong, then the right, side.

HAND APPLIQUÉ

1. Shapes that appear closest to the background fabric or that will have other shapes extending over part of them are positioned first. This generally applies to stems. Position the preshaped stems one at a time over the marked lines on the background fabric. Pin and then baste them in place.

2. Stitch them to the background fabric with a back whipstitch along both sides. See Glossary for help, if needed. If shapes will be machine appliquéd, proceed to the following section on Machine Appliqué.

3. Leaves are attached next. One at a time, pin, then baste, the leaves into position on the background fabric.

4. Starting on a curved side of the leaf, not at its point, stitch it in place using the back whipstitch. Stitch right up to the point. At the point, use the tip of your needle or your small scissors to tuck the excess fabric under the point. Take one extra, tiny stitch to hold it in place. Stitch around the opposite side, repeating the procedure at the other point and continuing around the curve, stopping ½″ (1.5 cm) from the starting point.

5. Remove the basting threads.

6. Use your tweezers to reach into the opening and remove the paper pattern.

7. Sew up the opening. End the stitching with two small backstitches on the wrong side.

8. Some small shapes are combined with larger shapes to form one unit before applying them to the background fabric, for example, centers to flowers or small buds to leaves. Place the smaller shape on the larger shape with their grainlines parallel. Hand stitch the small shape in place using a back whipstitch, stopping in time to remove the paper pattern.

9. Flowers with or without centers are placed on next. Pin, and then baste, the flowers in place.

10. Stitch the flowers to the background fabric using a back whipstitch,

stitching all the way around the shape. End with two small backstitches on the wrong side. Remove the basting threads.

11. Turn the design to the wrong side. Cut out the background fabric underneath the flower to within ¼″ (0.75 cm) of the stitching line. This is done on any large shape to eliminate excess bulk and prevent one color from shadowing through to another.

12. Finally, place the block, wrong side up, on a light-colored towel. Press firmly. Turn the block right side up and press lightly.

MACHINE APPLIQUÉ

Prepared shapes can also be machine appliquéd to the background fabric.

1. Either hand baste or fuse the prepared shape to the right side of the background fabric.

2. Stitch around the edge of the shape using one of the decorative stitches such as the buttonhole stitch on your sewing machine.

3. Remove any basting stitches.

4. If freezer paper was used, cut away the background fabric on the wrong side to within ¼″ (0.75 cm) of the stitching line. Then use the tip of your scissors or seam ripper to peel away and remove the freezer paper.

PRACTICE EXERCISE: Making a 12″ (30 cm) *Benicia Rose* Block

Adele Ingraham

1. Make a photocopy or trace the entire design onto a piece of paper. The design can be found on page 168.

2. Using this paper, trace all shapes needed onto another piece of plain paper and cut them out, using paper scissors. Mark the lengthwise grain line on each paper piece. Complete "Preparing the Pattern".

3. Cut a 12½″ (31.5 cm) square of background fabric, marking "Top" and grainline. Mark the placement of the shapes on the right side. Complete "Preparing and Marking the Background Fabric".

4. Make the stems as described in "Preparing Stems".

5. Pin and baste the individual paper shapes to the appropriate fabric. See "Pinning and Basting Paper Patterns to Fabric".

6. Pin, baste, and sew the individual shapes to the background fabric in the following sequence, removing the paper pattern after each application: stems, leaves, flowers.

7. Press the completed block firmly on its wrong side, then lightly on its right.

Chapter 7

FINISHING THE QUILT TOP

Congratulations! You have finished your quilt blocks. Now, as you piece them together to complete your quilt top, their beauty will be enhanced by new designs created from the combinations of blocks. This is the point at which your hard work literally comes together to create the beautiful quilt top you chose to make. In our classes, this is one of the most exciting times as students have an opportunity to see the impressive results of their work, share in each other's satisfaction, and get ideas for future quilts they would like to make.

Before you sew the quilt blocks together, check to see that the blocks are "squared-up" (all the same size). If you are making 12″ (30 cm) blocks, they should all measure 12½″ (31.5 cm). If one is a little too small, place a pin in it to remind yourself to compensate when you set the blocks together. Read the descriptions of the different types of sets below and experiment to see which setting you like best.

If you are making a *sampler* quilt, you will want to organize your blocks by color to achieve a pleasing result. *Helpful Hint:* To do this, put the blocks up on a wall that has been covered with a piece of polyester felted fleece or a piece of white flannel (this design board allows the blocks to stick, and you can move them around easily). Visually, you see things better if they are vertical. You will be able to make better judgments. First pick up the blocks, not arranging them in any particular order, and place them on the wall. Next, take your reducing glass, step back four steps or so, and look at the arrangement. Choose the blocks that jump out at you, the ones that attract your attention. These blocks usually fall into one or more of the following categories: very dark, dark and light contrast, bright and bold, and yellow and red. Place these blocks in the center of the quilt or in the four corners. Use the remainder of the blocks to fill in the spaces, balancing color and design.

STRAIGHT SETS

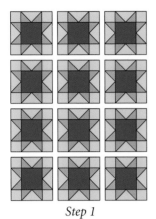

Step 1

Step 2

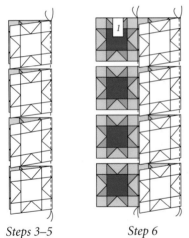

Steps 3–5   *Step 6*

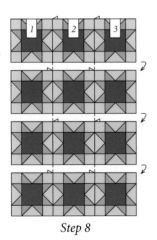

Step 8

In a straight set, the quilt blocks are sewn together in vertical and horizontal rows.

1. Lay out all the quilt blocks on the floor or on your design board in the desired arrangement. Look at the entire set (all of your blocks) through the reducing glass. This will help you correct any errors. When you are satisfied with the arrangement, pin pieces of paper, marked #1, #2, #3, etc., on the first block in each vertical row. Horizontal rows are indicated with letters. *Helpful Hint:* At this time, if any block is significantly too small, add a 1" (2.5 cm) frame of your background fabric, then trim the block to the needed size.

2. Pick up Block 1A and place it on top of Block 1B; then place these two on top of Block 1C, then 1D, etc. When you have completed this stack, repeat for Rows 2, 3, etc.

3. Take the stack of blocks in Rows 1 and 2 to the sewing machine. Place Block 2A on top of 1A, right sides together. Stitch them together on the right-hand edge.

4. Without breaking the thread, place Block 2B on top of 1B and feed them through the machine right behind the previous pair.

5. Repeat this procedure for the remainder of the blocks in Rows 1 and 2. *Do not cut the threads holding the blocks together.*

6. Pick up the stack of Row 3 blocks. With the right sides together, place Block 3A on top of Block 2A and stitch them together along the right-hand edge. Repeat for the remainder of the blocks in Row 3, continuing to chain them through the machine.

7. Add the stack of Row 4 blocks, then Row 5 blocks, etc., until all the blocks have been sewn together.

8. Press the new seams in Row A in one direction; press the new seams in Row B in the opposite direction. Continue pressing Rows C, D, etc., alternating the pressed direction of the seams.

9. Fold Row A face down on top of Row B. Pin them together at the intersections of their seams. Ease or stretch the blocks to fit, if necessary. The seams were pressed in opposite directions so they will lock in place. Stitch these rows together, being careful to check that the seam lines of the blocks match up.

10. Fold Row B face down on top of Row C and repeat the procedure. Repeat for the remaining rows.

11. The quilt blocks are now all sewn together and form a quilt top. Give them a final pressing, then proceed to the section on adding borders.

DIAGONAL SETS

When the quilt blocks are turned on point and sewn together, this is called a diagonal set. All the blocks must be laid out on the floor or on a design board, so you can view them through the reducing glass to see the complete design before sewing and thereby avoid mistakes.

You will note that side triangles are necessary to square up the quilt around the edges. The fabric used for these triangles can be one already used in the blocks or something entirely different, which will give the feeling that the blocks are suspended in space.

MAKING SIDE TRIANGLES

1. When all the quilt blocks are laid out on the floor, count to see how many side triangles are necessary (do not include corners).

Total number of triangles	(a)_____
Divide this number by 4	(b)_____
Round up to the nearest whole number. This gives the number of squares of fabric to cut.	
Take diagonal measurement of a block	(c)_____
Add 2″ (5 cm)	
Total	(d)_____

2. Cut the number of squares of fabric written on line (b) to the measurement written on line (d).

3. Cut the squares in quarters diagonally.

4. Lay these triangles around the edges of the quilt.

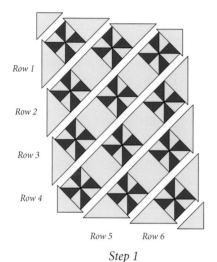

Row 1
Row 2
Row 3
Row 4
Row 5   *Row 6*

Step 1

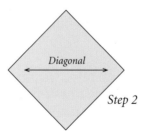

Diagonal

Step 2

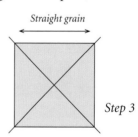

Straight grain

Step 3

MAKING CORNER TRIANGLES

1. Cut two squares of fabric the size of your block plus 1½″ (4.5 cm), i.e., if your blocks measure 12″ (30 cm), cut two 13½″ (34.5 cm) squares. Cut these in half diagonally.

2. Lay these triangles out on the floor in the corners of the quilt.

Note: Making side and corner triangles in this manner will result in a straight grain of fabric running around the entire edge of the quilt. This is important, as there will be less stretch than if triangles were cut on the bias, as is sometimes done. *Helpful Hint:* These triangles will all be a little too big, but the excess will be cut away when a border or binding is attached.

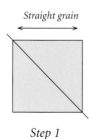

Straight grain

Step 1

ASSEMBLING THE QUILT TOP

1. With a piece of paper, mark diagonal Rows 1, 2, 3, 4, etc. These rows *will include the side triangles.*

2. Stitch the blocks in Row 1 together, then Row 2, etc.

3. Press the new seams in Row 1 in one direction. Press the new seams in Row 2 in the opposite direction. Repeat for the remaining rows, alternating the direction of the new seams.

4. Placing pins at the seam intersections, stitch Row 1 to Row 2. Then add Row 3, then Row 4, etc.

5. Sew on the four corner triangles.

6. Since your side triangles are too large, the sides of the quilt top need to be trimmed and straightened before you add borders. Take the quilt top to the cutting board and use the wide plastic ruler and rotary cutter to straighten the edges of the quilt and remove the excess fabric. *Helpful Hint:* Check to see that opposite sides are the same measurement and that the corners are at right angles.

7. Give the quilt top a final pressing before adding the borders.

DESIGN OPTIONS

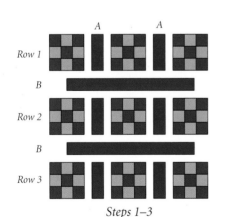

Row 1

B

Row 2

B

Row 3

A   A

Steps 1–3

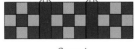

Step 4

Steps 5–6

ALTERNATE BLOCKS

One quick and easy way of enlarging your quilt and reducing the total number of pieced or appliquéd blocks is with the use of alternate blocks. The easiest alternate blocks are plain blocks set between the pieced or appliquéd blocks. They can be used in either a straight or a diagonal setting. See the *Bear's Paw* quilt on page 53, and the *Pine Tree* quilt on page 50 as examples of quilts with alternate blocks.

SASHING

Strips of fabric or sashing separate and frame the individual blocks. See the *Sawtooth Star* quilt on page 40. To use sashing in your quilt:

1. Lay all the quilt blocks on the floor or design board in the desired arrangement.

2. Determine the number of A and B strips necessary.

3. Cut all the A strips to the desired finished width plus ½″ (1.5 cm) seam allowance. The length of these strips will be the same measurement as the blocks.

4. Sew the A strips between the blocks in Row 1. Repeat for the remaining rows. Press the seams in the direction of the A strips.

5. Measure across Row 1. Using this measurement, cut the required number of B strips.

6. Lay a B strip on top of the bottom edge of Row 1, right sides together. Sew.

7. In the same way, sew a B strip to the bottom of all but one (last) row.

8. Pin Row 2 to the B strip of Row 1, being *very careful* to keep the A strips in a line. Ease in any fullness if necessary while sewing in order to keep the strips straight.

9. Continue the same process with the remainder of the rows.

10. Give the completed quilt top a final press.

Note: When sashing is used in a diagonal setting, add the width of the sashing to the diagonal measurement when determining the size of the side and corner triangles.

POSTS

Pieces of fabric join sashing to sashing at the intersection of the blocks. See the *Heart* quilt on page 60. To use posts in your quilt:

1. Lay all the blocks on the floor or your design board to determine the total number of sashing strips and posts needed.

2. Complete Steps 3 and 4 in the sashing instructions.

3. Use the width measurement of the sashing strips to cut squares of fabric for the required number of posts.

4. Cut the B sashing strips to the desired finished width plus ½" (1.5 cm) seam allowance.

5. For each row, sew the B strips to the posts, as shown in the diagram. Press the seams in the direction of the B strips.

6. Lay one of these finished B strips on top of the bottom of Row 1, right sides together. Align the posts in your B strip with the A strips and secure with pins. Sew.

7. In the same way, sew a B strip to the bottom of all but one (the last) row.

8. Pin Row 2 to the B strip of Row 1, being *very careful* to match all posts with their A strips. Ease in any fullness if necessary while sewing in order to keep the strips straight.

9. Continue the same process for the remainder of the rows.

10. Give the quilt top a final press.

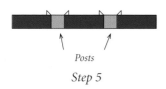

Posts

Step 5

Step 6

ADDING BORDERS

Borders affect the total design of the quilt. Often, even experienced quilt-makers give too little attention to the question of borders and to the selection of border designs and fabric. A simple geometric pattern can be enhanced by a border. Likewise, a complex, well-crafted quilt top can lose much of its appeal if the border is not carefully selected.

A border can appear as a separate frame for the quilt top; it can repeat colors, fabrics, or patterns from the quilt top, wholly or in part; or it may combine several of these traits. When you have completed your quilt top, pin it up on a design board and look at it through your reducing glass. This allows you to experiment with borders and see their relationship in size and pattern to the quilt top.

There are many different types of borders from which to choose. Look through the quilts in Chapter 1 for ideas or design your own. Remember:

1. A border can enhance a rather simple pattern to make it more interesting. See the *Fence Rail* quilt on page 16.

2. Repeating a color or fabric design used in the quilt top can help to unify your quilt. See the *Thousand Pyramids* quilt on page 58.

3. Wide borders of an unrelated fabric will add interest and texture. See the *Double Nine-Patch Variation* quilt on page 26.

4. Some patterns are complete in design without a border (see the *Log Cabin* quilt on page 18) and, sometimes, a border is a distraction, not an asset.

5. A border can be a single strip of fabric (see the *Attic Windows* quilt on page 42) or multiple strips of fabric (see the *All Stars* quilt on page 82). There are no set rules as to the number and width of borders.

6. Borders can be pieced, as in the sawtooth border around the *Bear's Paw* quilt on page 53: It is made simply from half-square triangles. The border on the *Madison House* quilt on page 46 is another option.

Your borders can be either straight or mitered. The difference between the two lies in the treatment of the corners. Either method is acceptable; it is simply a matter of preference. Often the type of border you choose will dictate the method of attachment. For example, you would generally not miter a pieced border.

DETERMINING AMOUNT OF FABRIC FOR BORDERS

The amount is based on fabric that is 42″ to 44″ (106 cm to 112 cm) selvage to selvage.

Straight Borders

CUTTING

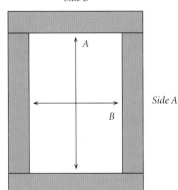

SIDE A

1. Dimension A, through center of quilt   _____

2. Working allowance: add 4″ (10 cm)   _____

3. For sides A, you will need 2 strips, each   _____

SIDE B

4. Dimension B, through center of quilt   _____

5. Width of border × 2   _____

6. Total (Steps 4 + 5)   _____

7. Working allowance: add 4″ (10 cm)   _____

8. For sides B, you will need 2 strips, each   _____

FABRIC

BORDER WIDTH	TOTAL FABRIC REQUIRED	
0″–11″ (0 cm–28 cm)	Larger of Step 3 or Step 8 ÷ 36″ (100 cm)	_____
11⅛″–22″ (28.5 cm–56 cm)	Steps 3 + 8 ÷ 36″ (100 cm)	_____

Mitered Borders

CUTTING

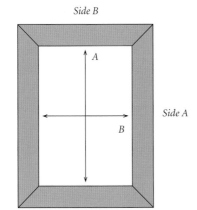

Side B

A

B

Side A

SIDE A

1. Dimension A, through center of quilt	_____
2. Width of border × 2	_____
3. Total (Steps 1 + 2)	_____
4. Working allowance: add 2″ (5 cm)	
5. For sides A, you will need 2 strips, each	_____

SIDE B

6. Dimension B, through center of quilt	_____
7. Width of border × 2	_____
8. Total (Steps 6 + 7)	_____
9. Working allowance: add 9″ (23 cm)	
10. For sides B, you will need 2 strips, each	_____

FABRIC

BORDER WIDTH	TOTAL FABRIC REQUIRED	
0″–11″ (0 cm–28 cm)	Step 5 ÷ 36″ (100 cm)	_____
11⅛″–22″ (28.5 cm–56 cm)	Steps 5 + 10 ÷ 36″ (100 cm)	_____

CUTTING BORDERS

1. It is best to cut the borders on the lengthwise grain of the fabric, as there is less stretch. Therefore, using your cutting tools, remove one selvage edge from the fabric. Since you are working with a lot of fabric for the border, you may not be able to fit the entire length on the board. Cut as much as possible and then move the fabric to cut the rest.

2. Place your wide plastic ruler on top of the fabric to measure, and cut four strips the desired border width plus ½″ (1.5 cm) for seam allowances, adjusting the ruler along the length as you cut. If you are using a directional fabric or a border-printed fabric, take care to cut straight along the printed pattern.

3. Repeat for any additional borders.

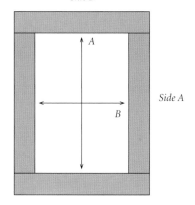

Side B

Side A

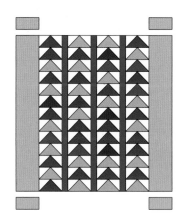

Step 6

ATTACHING STRAIGHT BORDERS

1. Lay the quilt top out on a flat surface and use the plastic or metal tape measure to determine dimensions A (the longer dimension) and B (the shorter dimension) across the center. Write these figures down.

2. You will be fitting the quilt top to the border strips *rather than* the border strips to the quilt top. This will prevent the edges of the borders from rippling. For best results, place pins at the center points of two border strips. Measure out from the pins in each direction a distance equal to half the A dimension. Place pins at these points to mark the corners.

3. Place pins at the center points along sides A of the quilt top.

4. Lay these border strips on each A side of the quilt top, right sides together, matching pins with corners and at the center points. Use more pins to hold the borders in place. Sew with the border strips on top, as they are less likely to stretch than the pieced quilt top. Ease in any fullness as necessary.

5. Press the fabrics flat to set the stitches in place. Fold the border strips back, over the stitching lines. Press them.

6. Use your cutting tools to trim the excess length of border fabric even with the B sides of the quilt top.

7. Mark the two remaining border strips and the B sides of the quilt top with pins at their center points. Measure out from the pins in each direction on the border strips, a distance equal to one-half the B dimension. Place pins at these points to mark the corners.

8. Attach these border strips to the quilt top using the same method described in Steps 4 and 5.

9. Use your cutting tools to trim the excess length of border fabric even with the A sides of the quilt top. Press on the right side.

Additional borders can be added if desired, using the same technique. *Always complete one border before adding another.* Your quilt top is now ready to be marked and layered for quilting or tying.

ATTACHING CORNER BLOCKS

A design option in planning borders is to add a corner block. This can solve problems if you are finding it difficult to turn the corner with pieced borders or if you do not have enough material length to miter the corners. A corner block can be the missing design element that adds that needed sparkle to your overall design. See the *All Stars* quilt on page 82.

1. Do steps 1 to 6 in "Attaching Straight Borders".

2. Cut the two B border strips using the B dimension determined in Step 1 of that section.

3. Use the width measurement of the B border strips to cut squares of fabric for the corner blocks.

4. Sew a corner block to each end of the B border strips.

5. Place pins at the center points of sides B of the quilt top and the B border strips.

6. Refer to Steps 4 and 5 of "Attaching Straight Borders," matching up the seams at the corner blocks with the seams of the A border strips.

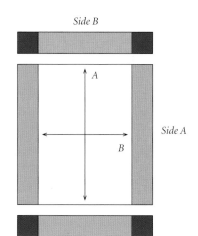

Side B

Side A

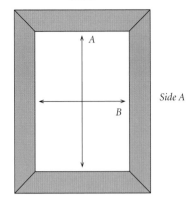

Side B

Side A

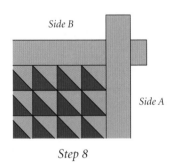

Side B

Side A

Step 8

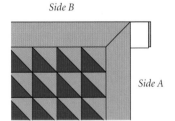

Side B

Side A

Step 9

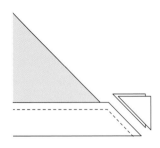

Step 12–13

ATTACHING MITERED BORDERS

When more than one border is desired, match the center points of the borders to each other. Sew together lengthwise in one unit before sewing to the quilt top. Treat this unit as one border strip and use the technique described here.

1. Using your plastic or metal tape measure, determine dimensions A and B of the quilt top across its center. Write these figures down.

2. You will be fitting the quilt top to the border strips *rather than* the border strips to the quilt top. This will prevent the edges of the borders from rippling. To achieve the best results, place pins at the center points of two border strips. Measure out from the pins in each direction a distance equal to one-half the A dimension. Place pins at these points to mark the corners.

3. Place pins at the center points along sides A of the quilt top.

4. Lay these border strips on each A side of the quilt top, right sides together, matching pins with corners and at the center points. Use more pins to attach the borders in place. Beginning and ending ¼″ *(0.75 cm) from each corner,* stitch the A borders to the quilt top, with the border strip on top, as it is more stable than the pieced quilt top and less likely to stretch. There will be a generous amount of fabric from both ends of the borders extending beyond the quilt top. This is needed to miter the corners. *Do not cut it off.*

5. Mark the center points on the two remaining border strips. Measure out from the pins in each direction a distance equal to one-half the B dimension. Place pins at these points to mark the corners.

6. Place pins at the center points along the B sides of the quilt top.

7. Using the method described in Step 4, sew the B borders to the B sides of the quilt top.

8. Take the quilt top to your pressing surface. Working on one corner of the quilt at a time, extend the unsewn border ends out straight, overlapping the end of A over the end of B.

9. Lift up the A border strip and fold it under *only itself,* at a 45° angle. The remainder of border A should lie even with both sides of the underlying B border.

10. Using your ruler with a 45° angle, check to see that the angle is accurate and the corner is square. Place pins to hold the border strips in place. Then press to set the angle.

11. Turn the quilt to the wrong side and place pins near the pressed fold in the corner to hold the border strips in place.

12. Take the quilt top to the sewing machine and, wrong side up, stitch along the folded line in the corner. Be careful to stitch right up to the previous stitching lines in the corner of the quilt top to avoid gaps.

13. Trim all excess fabric from the border strips.

14. Press on the right side.

15. Repeat for the remaining three corners.

Your quilt top is now ready to be marked and layered for quilting or tying.

ATTACHING BORDERS OF BORDER-PRINTED FABRIC

Border-printed fabrics are a quick and simple way of adding a new dimension to your quilt. It is important that the corners be the same, or at least that opposite corners match. Be sure to purchase extra fabric for matching. After the eye looks to the center of the quilt, it will be drawn out to the corners. These borders look best when the corners are mitered. If you are working on a square quilt, you will not have any difficulty in getting the designs to match in the corners, as long as you place a similar design at the center point of each side. A rectangular quilt is a little more challenging.

1. Use a metal or plastic tape measure to determine the A and B dimensions of the quilt top across the center. Write these figures down.

2. Place pins at the center points of each side of the quilt top.

3. You will be fitting the quilt top to the border strips *rather than* the border strips to the quilt top. This will prevent the edges of the borders from rippling. Choose a design in your border-printed fabric to be positioned at the center points of sides A of your quilt top. Mark it with pins. Measure out from the pins at these points to mark the corners. Do the same on the other A border strip.

4. Lay these border strips on each A side of the quilt top, right sides together, matching pins with corners and at the center points. Use more pins to keep the borders in place. Beginning and ending ¼″ (0.75 cm) from each corner, stitch the A borders to the quilt, with the border strips on top, as they more stable than the pressed quilt top and less likely to stretch. There will be a generous amount of fabric from both ends of the borders extending beyond the quilt top. This is needed to miter the corners. *Do not cut it off.*

5. Take the quilt top to the pressing surface and fold all four unsewn extensions of the borders back to form 45° angles. Check the accuracy of the angles with a ruler marked with a 45° angle. Press a fold in the angles.

6. Take the quilt top to a flat surface. Lay a B border strip along the B side of the quilt top. Line up the same design in the border fabric chosen in Step 3 with the center point of side B. The excess B border strip lengths must extend *under* the folded corners of the previously attached A border strips.

7. Pull the B border strip together at its center, forming a pleat. Watch the designs forming in the corners and continue pulling until you find one you like. Make sure you are pulling equal amounts from each end so that the corner designs will match each other. Now fold the pleat to the wrong side of the border strip and pin.

8. Repeat for the other B side of the quilt top.

9. Place pins in the corners to hold the A and B borders together.

10. Turn each B border strip right side down on the quilt top. Place pins along the edge to attach it to the quilt top, pinning from the corners to the center pleat.

11. Fold the quilt top in half lengthwise, right side out. The pleats will extend beyond the center folds in the quilt top.

Step 8

12. Stitch along each pleat even with the fold in the quilt top. Trim the excess to within ¼" (0.75 cm) of the stitching line. Press the seams in each B border strip to one side.

13. Unfold the quilt top and stitch your B border strips to it, beginning and ending ¼" (0.75 cm) from each corner.

14. To miter the corners, stitch along the folds which were pressed into the A border strips. For more details, see Steps 11 to 13 in "Attaching Mitered Borders."

15. Press on the right side.

Your quilt top is now ready to be marked and layered for quilting or tying.

PIECED BORDERS

Borders constructed from the repetition of a single shape or a combination of shapes are called pieced borders. The shapes often repeat some that have been used in the quilt top. The most difficult task in designing a pieced border is deciding how to turn the corners. The design must flow smoothly and the corners must be the same or, at least, opposite corners must be the same. Pieced borders, once constructed into strips, are attached using the same method described for straight borders. Specific instructions for the samples referred to here are given in Chapter 1.

Look at the *Bear's Paw* quilt on page 53. It has traditional sawtooth borders which zigzag around the edge of the quilt, causing the eye to travel to the outer edge.

A good example of repeating a shape used in the pattern block is the border of Diana and Laura's *Madison House* quilt on page 46. The fabrics have been stripped and then cut, repeating the rectangular shapes in the houses.

The *Star of Bethlehem* quilt on page 78 uses a small *Sawtooth Star* in its border. Although both are stars, they are constructed of different shapes.

Sometimes you may want a border unrelated to the pattern. This causes the border to stand apart. Look at the *Pineapple Log Cabin* quilt on page 68, covering the border with plain paper to hide it. Now, remove the paper and see how the border adds a feeling of fun and whimsy.

Chapter 8

ASSEMBLY

 Now that your quilt top is complete, you must give some thought to how you would like to finish the quilt. How would you like to secure the three layers (top, batting, and backing) of the quilt together? Your quilt can be handquilted, machine-quilted, or tied. Read through the description of each technique below, keeping in mind the amount of time you want to devote to finishing your quilt and how it will ultimately be used.

Hand quilting. Small running stitches hold the three layers together, either following lines or patterns that have been marked on the quilt top or following the outline of a pieced or appliquéd block, or both. Hand quilting gives strength, dimension, texture, and design to a quilt. It requires quite a bit of time and takes practice to make small, even stitches, but the result will be an heirloom.

Machine quilting. Machine stitches hold the three layers of the quilt together. As in hand quilting, the stitches follow a design which has been marked on the quilt top, or the stitches can be sewn in the seams around a pieced block. With some practice, you can achieve beautiful results.

Tying. Small square knots are taken through all layers to hold them together. This is the quickest method of finishing. It can also provide surface design. Sometimes, ribbon bows are added for decoration.

BACKING FABRIC

As with the quilt top, it is important to choose a good-quality cotton fabric for your backing. Although a bed sheet may seem to be a good idea because of its convenient size, it is *not* suitable because the fabric is too tightly woven and you will have difficulty quilting through it.

When choosing the fabric for the backing, be sure to select a color that will not show through on the front, especially if the quilt top contains light colors; a dark, bright, or bold print may show through. The backing can be a good opportunity to use a completely different fabric from those used on the top. Try something exciting for added interest. It is always fun to turn over a quilt and discover something unexpected.

Another option might be to piece the backing. It is a good way to use up some leftover lengths of fabric.

MEASUREMENT AND PREPARATION

The amount of fabric is based on bolts measuring 42″ to 44″ (106 cm to 112 cm) selvage to selvage.

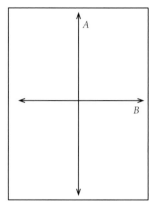

1. Lay the quilt top on a flat surface to determine A and B measurements.

2. You will want your cut backing fabric to be at least 2″ (4 cm) larger than the quilt top all the way around. Add 4″ (10 cm) for a "working allowance" to the A measurement. This is the measurement of one length.

3. Use this helpful chart to determine yardage for backing:

IF DIMENSION B IS	LENGTHS NEEDED
0″– 40″ (0 cm – 96 cm)	1
41″– 80″ (97 cm – 203 cm)	2
81″– 120″ (204 cm – 305 cm)	3

4. If two or three lengths are required, cut the selvage edges off the lengths and stitch them together along the longer sides with a ¼″ (0.75 cm) seam. Press the seam(s) to one side for machine quilting or press open for hand quilting.

BATTING

Batting is the filling layer between the quilt top and the backing. Battings can be purchased in various weights, either prepackaged and cut to a specified size or by the yard (meter). There are also different types of batting. Look at the thickness before purchasing it. A thin batting will be easier to work with in hand quilting and give a more traditional look to your quilt, whereas a thicker batting is more suitable for machine quilting or tying and gives a down-like appearance. It is important to purchase a good-quality batting. The inexpensive battings may be too stiff and lose their resilience after washing. We advise that you purchase a batting that is soft, uniform in thickness, and without lumps.

TYPES OF BATTING

100% Cotton or Cotton/Polyester Blends
A pure cotton batting with a low loft or a blend will give a traditional

appearance to your finished quilt. It will require you to do very close quilting, with no more than 1″ (1.5 cm) between quilting lines, to achieve maximum durability in the quilt. Cotton batting has a tendency to shift and pull away if it is not quilted closely, causing it to lump. This batting can be used for either hand or machine quilting. An advantage to cotton batting is that it is nonallergenic and resists fiber migration. Fiber migration occurs when the tiny fibers of the batting surface creep through the quilt top, giving a lint-like appearance.

100% Polyester (Bonded)

The polyester battings can be purchased in various weights. The thicker batting will require less stitching but will be difficult for fine, even hand quilting. The low-loft or traditional polyester battings—less than ½″ (1.5 cm) thick—are suitable for hand quilting. The very heavy lofts and thick battings—more than ½″ (1.5 cm) thick—are used for tied quilts. But, remember—polyester fibers migrate more easily than do cotton fibers, and this problem is particularly noticeable on dark fabrics.

PREPARING TO QUILT

Before proceeding, check to see if:

1. The quilt top is pressed flat and without wrinkles.

2. All quilting lines are marked.

3. The backing is ready.

4. You have batting, either precut or by the yard (buy the same number of lengths as you bought of backing fabric).

If so, you are ready to proceed with layering your quilt and basting the layers together in preparation for quilting or tying. Follow the instructions for the technique you have chosen.

QUILTING IN A HOOP: LAYERING AND BASTING

1. Lay the backing fabric out on a smooth, flat surface, wrong side up. You can use a large table, a large cutting board, or the floor. Do not use a good dining room table unless it is covered with a cloth and then a cutting board, because the needle will scratch the surface.

2. Pull the edges of the backing taut to eliminate any fullness or wrinkles, then tape it to your work surface. Tape the four center points first, then the four corners, keeping the edges as straight and the backing as square as possible. Add more tape around the edges.

3a. If you are using precut batting, place the roll in the center of the backing fabric and gently unfold it, covering the backing. Smooth out any folds or creases. The batting now covers the entire backing fabric.

—or—

3b. If using batting purchased by the yard (meter), you will need to butt the lengths together and, using a double strand of thread and a #1 cotton darning needle, sew them together with a diagonal basting stitch.

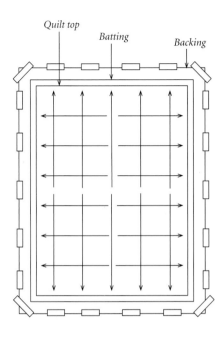

Quilt top Batting Backing

Place the batting on top of the backing and smooth out any folds.

4. Place the quilt top with the right side facing up on top of the batting, matching the center points of the quilt top to the center points marked on the backing fabric.

5. Pin through all layers with glass-head pins, starting in the center of the quilt and moving out to the edges. Place pins about 6″ (15 cm) apart. This will hold the layers together for hand basting.

6. With scissors, cut off the excess batting to within ½″ (1.5 cm) of all four of the quilt top sides.

7. Use a #1 cotton darning needle and cotton thread; cut a long length of thread—about 50″ (127 cm). Using a single thickness of thread with a knot in the end, start in the center of your quilt and work to the edge, making a long diagonal basting stitch to hold the layers together. Your stitches should form a 4″ (10 cm) grid.

8. Remove the masking tape and the pins. Fold the excess backing in half so that the raw edge of the backing comes up even with the raw edge of the quilt top. Fold the backing again, bringing the fold of backing over the edge of the quilt top ¼″ (0.75 cm). Secure the folded edge of the backing to the quilt top with glass-head pins all the way around the edge of the quilt. With a running basting stitch, sew this folded edge through all three layers, removing the pins as you sew. This is an important step, because it will protect the edge of the quilt top from stretching and raveling and prevent the batting from linting out while you are quilting.

You are now ready to proceed to Chapter 9 and begin hand quilting.

QUILTING IN A FRAME

Making and Using Your Own Quilt Frame

1. Fold pieces of muslin in half lengthwise with the raw edges even. The muslin should measure 5″ (10 cm) × width of backing.

2. Mark the center point on one of the wider sides of each of four boards, each measuring approximately ¾″ × 1½″ (2 cm × 4 cm), and about 12″ (30 cm) bigger than the quilt backing.

3. Place the muslin pieces on top of the boards, center points matched, with the raw edge of the muslin centered on the board. Staple the muslin to the boards, placing staples at about 2″ (5 cm) intervals: these muslin pieces are now your four header strips.

4. This requires two people. *Warning:* Do not attempt to do it alone. Using your right-angle triangle, place an A board and a B board at right angles, stapled sides up, and secure them in place with a clamp at the corner. Repeat for the remaining three corners. The distance between the corners should be the same as the backing fabric for the quilt.

5. The frame must be elevated and supported. You can balance the boards on top of four straight-backed chairs.

6. Find the center points on the four header strips and mark them with glass-head pins. Also mark the center points on the four sides of the backing fabric.

7. With the wrong side of the backing fabric facing up, match the cen-

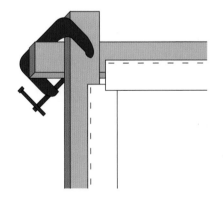

ter points of the backing fabric to the center points of the header strips. Use pins to secure the backing to the header strips at these four points.

8. Using pins, secure the four corners of the backing to the header strips, measuring from the center points out to the corners to be sure that the distance is the same on each side.

9. Secure the rest of the backing to the header strips, easing in any fullness if necessary.

10a. If you are using precut batting, place the batting in the center of the backing and gently unfold it to cover the backing. Smooth out any folds.
—OR—

10b. If you are using batting purchased by the yard (meter), you will need to butt the lengths together and, using a double strand of thread and a #1 cotton darning needle, sew them together with a diagonal basting stitch. Place the batting on top of the backing and smooth out any folds.

11. Place pins at the center points on the four sides of the quilt top. Lay the quilt top on top of the batting, with the right side facing up, matching the center points with those on the header strips. (The quilt top will be smaller than the batting and backing but the center points should line up.)

12. Measure from the center points to the corners of the quilt top, making sure the distances on opposite sides are the same, and pin the quilt top through the batting and backing all around the edges. *Warning:* This is an important step. Double-check to see that the pinned quilt top is squared off and even; otherwise, your finished quilt will not be straight.

13. Make running basting stitches around the edge of the quilt through all three layers, removing the pins as you sew.

Using a Ready-Made Frame
Follow the instructions that accompany your frame, using any of the instructions and hints that will work to help you.

You are now ready to move on to Chapter 9 and begin hand quilting.

MACHINE QUILTING

1. Complete Steps 1 to 4 under "Quilting in a Hoop" and prepare your quilt in the same manner.

2. Place #1 steel safety pins no more than 3" (7 cm) apart throughout the entire quilt. Start pinning the center of the quilt and work out toward the edges. Be careful not to place the pins where you intend to stitch.

3. With scissors, cut off the excess batting to within ½" (1.5 cm) of all four of the quilt top sides.

You are ready to move on to Chapter 9 and begin machine quilting.

TYING

A quilt can be tied either on a flat surface or in a frame. If you wish to use a flat surface as a table or the floor, prepare the quilt as instructed in Steps 1 to 6 of "Quilting in a Hoop." If you have a frame to use for tying, prepare the quilt as instructed in Steps 1 to 12 of "Quilting in a Frame."

Proceed to Chapter 9 for instructions for tying your quilt.

Chapter 9

QUILTING

Many of our quilting students tell us that they find the time spent in quilting to be soothing. The relaxed, rhythmic motion of stitching is a calming contrast to our usual hectic, fast-paced lives. This leisurely activity allows quilters some quiet moments to get in touch with their feelings and thoughts.

Whereas many of the piecing techniques are quick, the hand-quilting experience is not: even our most reluctant students admitted that they found the hand-quilting experience to be very rewarding; they were pleased with their work and proud they had stuck with it. All the students were eager to share their work with fellow students, family members, and friends. They found the praise they received for their hard work very gratifying.

Although three methods of completing your quilt are included in this chapter, we strongly recommend that at some point you devote some time to hand quilting. We feel that, in doing so, you will experience a new sense of yourself and share in the heartfelt tradition of hand quilting.

CHOOSING AND PLANNING THE QUILTING DESIGN

Whether you have decided to hand or machine quilt, you will need to choose a quilting design. Give as much attention to the selection of the design as you did to the construction of your quilt. Keep in mind that quilting shows up more on solid fabrics than on prints.

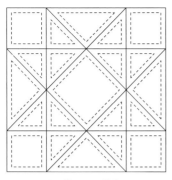

Outline Quilting

Background Quilting

Design Quilting

Border Design

OUTLINE QUILTING

This follows the outline on either or both sides of a pieced or appliquéd block. Stitches can be made either very close to the seam line or ⅛″ to ¼″(0.4 cm to 0.75 cm) away. The outline quilting accentuates the shape. The shape around which you quilt will appear to come forward.

BACKGROUND QUILTING

This quilting fills large, often plain, spaces that you wish to make recede visually, allowing the more important patterns and designs to come forward. Our favorite background quilting lines are crossed diagonal lines because they are easy to make with a straight-edge ruler and simple to quilt.

DESIGN QUILTING

These designs (such as wreaths, feathers, cables, and baskets) work well in open spaces like alternate blocks, side and corner triangles, and border areas. They are often combined with background quilting. See the *Star of Bethlehem* quilt on page 78. There are many plastic quilting design templates available, including special ones for corners. Look for a design that appeals to you, relates well to the pattern of your quilt, and fits nicely into the space you wish to quilt.

MARKING THE QUILTING DESIGNS ON THE QUILT TOP

Once you have selected your quilting designs, you will have to mark them on your quilt top. This is done before the quilt is layered and basted. It can be a tedious job and takes a bit of planning and time. *Do not rush through this step.*

If you are planning to outline quilt, you can either stitch close to the seam line or stitch ⅛″ to ¼″ (0.4 cm to 0.75 cm) away from it. If you are going to stitch close, you will not have to mark the quilting line. If you wish to quilt ¼″ (0.75 cm) away from your seam line you can use a ¼″ (0.75 cm) square Plexiglas rod to mark the quilting line.

If you have decided on a design for the border (such as a cable or feather), you will want the design to flow smoothly around the corner. Begin marking the corners and work toward the center of the border. *Helpful Hint:* Cut a strip of paper the exact size of the border, from the center point of one side to the center point of the other side (corner included). Trace the design onto the paper. You will be able to see where adjustments are needed before marking your fabric.

Keep a pencil sharpener close by. Use an artist's pencil (white, gray, or silver) for marking the lines on your quilt top. Test the marking pencil on a scrap of fabric before starting to mark on your quilt. Do *not* use water-soluble or disappearing marking pens: the ink may transfer into the batting and eventually reappear on the quilt top.

Place a piece of ultra-fine sandpaper under the area of your quilt to be marked. This prevents the fabric from slipping and the pencil from dragging. As lightly as possible but visibly, mark the desired quilting line. Mark all the quilting lines on the entire quilt top.

HAND QUILTING

If you are quilting on a frame, begin quilting along the edges of the quilt and work in toward the center. If you are quilting in a hoop, begin your quilting stitches in the center of the quilt and move to the edges. There are various sizes and shapes of hoops to choose from. *Helpful Hint:* Purchase a size that feels comfortable to you, so that it is neither too small nor too large. We have had success working in a 14″ (36 cm) hoop. A good-quality wooden hoop is advised. Place the smaller ring of the hoop on a table. With the right side of the quilt facing up, position the area to be quilted on top of the smaller ring. Next, loosen the screw in the larger ring and lay it on top of the quilt, gently pushing it over the smaller ring. Smooth out any wrinkles in the quilt. Tighten up the screw in the larger ring to secure the quilt in place. The quilt should be neither too tight nor too loose in the hoop. You are ready to begin the quilting stitch.

THE QUILTING STITCH

There are two methods for beginning the quilting stitch, the Knot Method and the No-Knot Method. The Knot Method works well if you are doing a lot of straight-line quilting without many starting and stopping points. The No-Knot Method works well on quilting designs such as wreaths, feathers, or others with several starting and stopping points.

The Knot Method

Step 3

1. Cut a length of quilting thread approximately 24″ (60 cm) long.

2. Using a needle threader if necessary, thread your fine, short Betweens needle, and hold it with the point upward.

3. To make a knot, hold the cut end of the thread between your index finger and the needle. Wrap the thread around the needle twice. Hold the thread in place with your fingers.

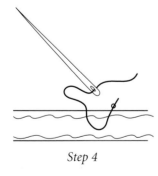

Step 4

4. Without pulling so hard as to unthread the needle, carefully release the thread from between your fingers and slide the thread down and off the needle all the way to the other end of the thread. A knot should form at the end of the thread. This is a good method for making knots because it keeps them uniform in size.

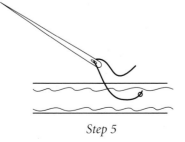

Step 5

5. Starting ½″ (1.5 cm) away from the line you wish to quilt, stick the needle down through the quilt top and into the batting layer only. Do not go through to the backing. Bring the needle up on the line you wish to quilt. Gently pull on the thread. The knot will be lying on the top of the quilt.

6. In order to hide the knot in the batting layer, gently tug on the thread with one hand and roll the thumbnail of the other hand over the top of the knot. This causes the knot to pop down into the batting layer.

7. Begin the quilting stitch with a very short backstitch.

8. Put on your thimble, take one small stitch with the thimble finger, going down all the way through the backing and up, working only on the tip of the needle. Place two fingers of the opposite hand underneath the quilt in order to feel the point of the needle as it goes down, and quickly push it to return it to the top. A quick return gives a small stitch. This should be done in a rocking motion—down-up-down-up-down-up— picking up about four stitches on the tip of the needle. Push the needle through. (Use a rubber thumb or a finger cot at this point if it is difficult to bring the needle through.) *Helpful Hint:* After you have pulled the thread taut, give just a little tug to move the position of the needle on the thread. This will prevent the thread from shredding at the eye of the needle. This is a very good habit to get into.

9. Repeat this step, picking up another four small stitches on the tip of the needle. Make the stitches as small as possible without worrying too much about the length. As you are quilting, make certain you clip your basting stitches so you do not quilt over them. It will take about three hours of *continual* quilting to break through what we call "the quilting barrier." At this point, the stitching will become even smaller, less of a conscious effort and more of a pleasure. It is important to stick with it and try to relax to avoid getting a pain in your upper back and neck area. *Helpful Hint:* In order to keep eyestrain to a minimum, raise your eyes and look away from your work at least once every fifteen minutes.

10. When there is about 5″ (12 cm) of thread left on the needle, take a small backstitch, bringing the needle through the loop that is formed. Now, pull the thread tight to create a knot.

11. Stick the needle into the same hole as the knot, going down into the batting layer, and give a little tug to pop the knot down. Come up to the top approximately ½″ (1.5 cm) away. Take another very small backstitch and stick the needle down again; this time, come up ¼″ (0.75 cm) away and cut the thread off.

The No-Knot Method

1. Cut a length of quilting thread approximately 36″ (90 cm) long.

2. Thread the needle, using a needle threader if necessary.

3. Stick the needle up through the three layers and pull up only half of the thread. Leave the other half hanging. You will work with only one half at a time.

4. Take a small backstitch and continue with the quilting stitches as already described. End as in Steps 10 and 11 of The Knot Method.

5. Return to your starting point and thread the tail that was left hanging. Take a small backstitch and continue with the quilting stitches in the opposite direction, ending as in The Knot Method. If you are using a hoop, reposition it as necessary.

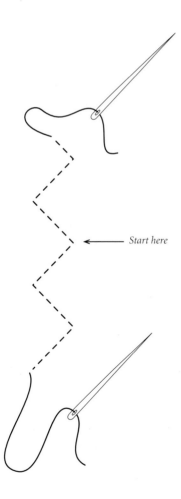

Start here

Most beginning quilters have a tendency to quilt around small shapes, one at a time. It is, however, faster and more efficient to quilt in one direction with long continuous lines.

With the quilting thread, measure along the line you wish to quilt, add 4″ (10 cm) to the measurement and cut the thread. This will ensure that you will not run out of thread halfway along the stitching line. Your stitches will be easier to make if you stitch toward yourself and then turn or angle toward the left-hand side (reverse for left-handed people). When you reach a seam intersection, slip the needle and thread under and beyond the seam allowances, into the batting layer, and bring the needle up at the next area to be quilted. Most intersections have thick seams which cause you to lose the rhythmic motion of the running stitches. You may need to take one or two stabs to get beyond the bulky seams. Then continue with the running stitch. If you are quilting a design with lines in two directions, or crossed directions, it will be helpful to thread two needles, working in one direction with one needle and in the opposite direction with the other needle.

Many people quilt ⅛″ to ¼″ (0.4 cm to 0.75 cm) away from each seam line. This forms an indentation on each side of the seam, raising the stitched seam. It will also strengthen the seam line and give durability to your quilt. It will be difficult to stitch closer than ¼″ (0.75 cm) on the side to which the seam allowance has been pressed, as there will be two additional layers of fabric to stitch through.

Helpful Hint: If you are quilting in a hoop and have finished for the day, remove the quilt from the hoop to avoid getting deep creases in it.

Proceed to Chapter 10 for instructions on attaching the binding.

MACHINE QUILTING

Machine quilting has gained popularity within the last few years. It is an excellent way to give design and texture to a quilt without devoting the many hours required for hand quilting. Machine quilting does not have to be limited to straight-line stitching. We recommend, however, that you try to tackle the more involved quilting patterns only after practice.

To machine quilt:

1. Attach an even-feed walking foot to your sewing machine. *Helpful Hint:* To prevent the thread from puckering or your quilt from not feeding evenly through the machine, check to see that the walking foot is fitted on the machine properly, with the bar resting on top of the needle bar of the machine.

2. Adjust the stitch length to 8 to 10 stitches per inch (3 to 4 stitches per cm). This is mark 2.5 on some models. *Helpful Hint:* Start with a full bobbin of thread. It is frustrating to run out of thread in the middle of a stitching line.

3. Now, lay the quilt out on a flat surface.

4. You will begin stitching near the center of one side, preferably on a seam line. Roll two opposite sides of the quilt toward the center, leaving the seam or stitching area exposed.

5. Starting from the bottom, roll the quilt up toward the top.

6. Place the quilt in the sewing machine and stitch along the center line or area to be quilted, unrolling the length of the quilt as you go. *Warning:* Be careful that this roll does not get caught up on your sewing table, preventing the quilt from feeding evenly through the machine.

7. Unroll the quilt, reroll it, and fold it to expose another area to be quilted. Continue until the entire quilt has been stitched. It is best to stitch all areas in one direction and then turn the quilt and stitch perpendicular to the first stitching lines.

8. Remove the safety pins.

Proceed to Chapter 10 for instructions on attaching the binding to your quilt.

TYING

At this point your quilt should be layered, on a flat surface or in a frame, ready to be tied. For best results, place your ties no more than 6″ (15 cm) apart.

1. Thread the darning needle with a double thickness length of perle cotton—cut about a 60″ (150 cm) length of thread. Do not knot the end.

2. Choose a point in the center of the quilt where you would like to make a tie. Poke the needle down through all thicknesses and come up approximately ⅛″ (0.5 cm) away.

3. Move to the next spot to be tied and take a small stitch.

4. Working in one direction, continue across the quilt until you have run out of thread. You will want to take the stitches all in one direction.

5. Rethread the needle and continue stitching until the quilt top is done.

6. With scissors, clip the threads between the stitches.

7. Tie a square knot at each point.

8. Trim off any excess thread if the tails are too long.

Proceed to Chapter 10 for instructions on attaching the binding.

Chapter 10

BINDING

 The final step in completing your quilt is the application of a binding. A binding is a narrow strip of fabric that is used as a finishing edge over the raw edges of the entire quilt, encasing its three layers. The edges of the quilt receive a lot of wear and tear; you might notice, in looking at older quilts, that the edge is usually the first part to wear out. Although there are several methods of binding a quilt, we like the method described here because it is quite durable and will give longer wear to your quilt; it involves wrapping *two* layers of fabric around the edge of your quilt.

PREPARING YOUR QUILT FOR BINDING

Many times, after your quilt has been quilted, either by hand or machine, it may no longer be square. The stitching lines may have stretched it a little out of shape. This occurs generally along the edges and in the corners. Now is the time to straighten it up.

1. Lay the quilt out on a flat surface, top side up.

2. Place pins perpendicular to the edge every 3″ (8 cm) through all layers to hold it flat. This step will also prevent any chance of the backing being cut too small.

4. Use your wide plastic ruler to straighten the edges and, with the rotary cutter, remove any excess batting and backing. Make sure the corners are at right angles. While you have the quilt flat, measure all four sides. Note the measurements, as you will need them later in "How to Determine the Length of Binding Strips."

3. Machine baste around the quilt top, through all thicknesses, approx-

imately ⅛″ (0.4 cm) from the edge. *Helpful Hint:* A walking foot on your sewing machine will provide even stitches.

BINDING YOUR QUILT

Binding strips can be cut on either the straight grain or the bias. Strips cut on the straight grain are easier to cut. Using them, a beginning quilter can easily achieve a finished edge without ripples. Left-over lengths of border or backing fabric can be used. Straight binding, however, is not appropriate for quilts with curved or zigzag edges.

A bias binding requires more care. It is important to sew slowly and *not* stretch the binding (to avoid rippled edges). An even-feed walking foot will be helpful. Bias binding is a must for quilts with curved or zigzag edges.

CHOOSING THE WIDTH OF BINDING STRIPS

The cut width of the fabric strips you will be using for straight or bias bindings is determined by the finished width of the binding. We prefer a very narrow—¼″ (0.75 cm)—finished binding on quilts that have thin, flat batting, whereas a wider—½″ (1.5 cm)—finished binding is easier to handle on quilts with thicker battings.

For a ¼″ (0.75 cm) finished binding, cut strips of fabric 1⅞″ (5 cm) wide.

For a ½″ (1.5 cm) finished binding, cut strips of fabric 3¼″ (9.5 cm) wide.

Helpful Hint: To cut bias strips, fold your fabric to form a 45° angle and cut.

HOW TO DETERMINE THE LENGTH OF BINDING STRIPS

To determine the cut length of straight binding strips, use the measurements from Step 3 under "Preparing Your Quilt for Binding." Take an average of two opposite side measurements. Now add 2″ (5 cm) and cut two strips this length. Repeat this process for the other two sides.

For a continuous bias binding, you must sew enough strips end-to-end to extend around the entire edge of the quilt. Add a 12″ (30 cm) working allowance.

ATTACHING BINDING STRIPS TO YOUR QUILT

Attaching a Straight Binding

1. Take one binding strip and fold it in half lengthwise, with the right side of the fabric on the outside. Mark the center point of the strip with a pin. Place a pin at the center point on an appropriate side of the quilt. Lay the binding strip on top of the quilt, lining up the raw edges of the binding strip with the raw edge of the quilt. Pin the binding strip to the

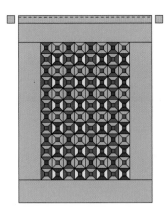

Step 2

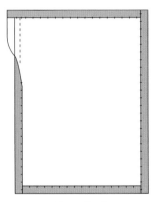

Steps 7– 8

Steps 2–3

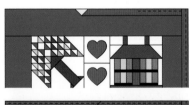

Step 4

quilt, matching up the center points and having 1″ (3 cm) of binding strip extend beyond the edge of the quilt at each end.

2. With the binding strip on the top, stitch through all thicknesses, from end to end, using a ¼″ (0.75 cm) seam allowance for narrow binding or ½″ (1.5 cm) seam allowance for wide binding. Ease in any fullness by pulling the binding taut while sewing. Trim off the excess 1″ (3 cm) from each end.

3. Fold the binding strip to the back side of the quilt and hand stitch it in place to the backing, using a small slip stitch.

4. Repeat this procedure for the opposite side of the quilt.

5. Next, attach the binding strips to the two remaining sides of the quilt using the same technique, except do not cut the excess 1″ (3 cm) from the edges of the binding strips. This excess is used to finish off the corners.

6. Flip the binding over the seam, then fold the 1″ (3 cm) excess under the quilt.

7. Hold the fold in place and fold the binding strip to the back of the quilt. Pin along the length of the strip. Now, hand stitch it in place to the backing, using a small slip stitch.

8. Repeat Steps 6 and 7 for each corner.

Attaching a Continuous Binding

You can begin binding anywhere along the edge of the quilt except in a corner. *Helpful Hint:* After you have selected a starting point, run the binding strip around the edge of the quilt to make certain that a seam does not fall into a corner. If it does, readjust your starting point.

1. Fold your bias strip in half lengthwise, right side out. Line up the raw edge of the strip with the raw edge of the quilt top.

2. Leaving a 4″ (10 cm) tail, stitch the binding to the quilt with a ¼″ (0.75 cm) seam allowance for narrow binding or ½″ (1.5 cm) seam allowance for wide binding. Stitch up to the seam line in the corner. Take a few backstitches. Remove the quilt from your sewing machine.

3. Diagonally fold the binding strip away from the quilt, as shown.

4. Fold the binding straight down, even with the edge of the quilt. Stitch. Continue and finish all sides and corners in the same manner. When you are within 4″ (10 cm) of your starting point, stop and remove the quilt from your machine. Slip the end of the binding strip into the starting end, as shown. Trim any excess. Stitch the final section of binding to the quilt.

5. Fold the binding to the wrong side and hand slip stitch it to the backing, stitching to the seam line in a corner. At the corner, fold the binding to form a miter. Continue stitching around the quilt, folding the remaining corners in the same manner.

Congratulations! You have successfully completed your quilt.

Chapter 11

DRAFTING PATTERNS

 Any quilt pattern can be drafted (an outline made of the shapes in the block) on a piece of graph paper. Once the pattern has been drafted, you can make individual pattern parts (called templates) from template plastic. Although we give template patterns for all the blocks included in this book except *Pineapple Log Cabin,* we feel that a lesson in drafting is good experience. It will give you confidence to reproduce other patterns and design your own. And it will give you the freedom to create pattern blocks in this book in sizes other than 12″ (30 cm) square.

Drafting is easier if you learn to examine the block and break it down into smaller divisions. Count the number of divisions across the top of the block and multiply that number by itself to determine the total number of squares in the block. This is called the grid and it can now be transferred onto a piece of graph paper.

THE GRID SYSTEM

For our purposes, a grid is a larger square broken down into smaller-squares of uniform size. Most traditional pieced quilt block patterns can be placed into categories based upon the grid system. With an understanding of the grid system, you will be better able to see and draft the individual shapes contained in most quilt block patterns.

Review the sample blocks shown to see how they have been divided. *Once you understand the concept, you will be able to draft patterns for any size finished block.* Divide the number of divisions across the top of the block into the desired finished size of the block to determine the measurement of each division. Each division can represent any measurement. You may want to make the finished size a little larger or smaller than you originally planned, to avoid working with difficult fractions.

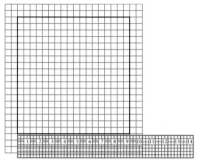

Step 2

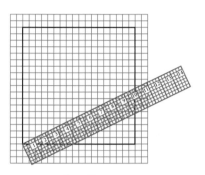

Step 3

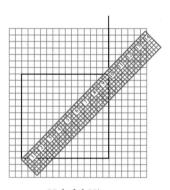

Helpful Hint

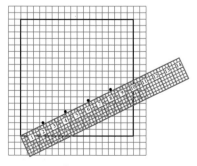

Step 4

MARKING A GRID

Drafting begins with marking an accurate square, the finished size of your block, onto a piece of graph paper. This is a simple task, as the graph paper provides a grid of squares of uniform size and accurate 90° angles. You can use a pencil and large C-Thru ruler to follow the guide lines on the paper. In most cases, once you have marked the outer edges of your block, you can simply follow the lines on the graph paper to fill in the individual template shapes. With a little practice, you will soon be able to examine a pieced block pattern, identify the grid category and draft the individual template shapes.

In most cases it will not be necessary to mark the outline of the grid. There are some instances, however, when the grid markings will not line up exactly with the graph paper. In these cases it will be helpful to mark the grid lines *before* filling in the individual shapes. Marking a grid is a relatively simple task. You would have no trouble marking a grid for a Five-Patch pattern (a pattern that divides into 25 equal squares) within a 10″ (25 cm) block. Each square of the grid will measure 2″ (5 cm) on each side.

Determining the size of each square within the grid is easy when the block is easily divisible by the grid size: for example, 10″ (25 cm) block size divided by 5 (number of squares across the grid) = 2″ (5 cm), the size of each square within the grid.

There may be an instance when you want to make a Five-Patch pattern in a 9″ (22 cm) block (or any other block size which is not easily divisible by 5). The following method will allow you to mark an accurate grid within any size block. This is a very useful and easy technique.

Using the example of a Five-Patch grid within a 9″ (22 cm) block:

1. Using a lead pencil and C-Thru ruler, mark a 9″ (22 cm) square onto a piece of graph paper.

2. Lay your large C-Thru ruler directly below the bottom edge of the square, with the left-hand edge in line with the bottom left-hand corner of the square, exactly as shown in the diagram.

3. Holding the upper left-hand corner of the ruler in place, carefully swing the right side of the ruler up until the 10″ (25 cm) marking intersects the right-hand edge of the square, exactly as shown in the diagram. Make sure the upper corner of the ruler is *exactly* at the corner. *Note:* 10″ (25 cm) is used because it is the next whole number greater than 9″ (22 cm) block size which is evenly divisible by 5 (number of squares across the grid).

Helpful Hint: If, when you swing the ruler, the next whole number extends beyond the right-hand edge of the square, you can extend the right-hand side of the square and place the ruler, exactly as shown in the diagram.

4. Using your pencil, mark points along the ruler every 2″ (5 cm), exactly as shown in the diagram. *Note:* 2″ (5 cm) is used because 10″ (25 cm) (next whole number determined in Step 3) divided by 5 (number of squares across the grid) = 2″ (5 cm).

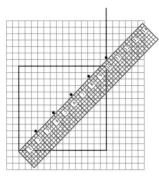

Helpful Hint

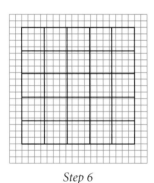

Step 5

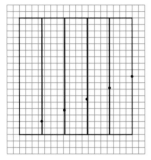

Step 6

Helpful Hint: If you are working with an extended right-hand edge, lay the ruler and mark points, exactly as shown in the diagram.

5. Keeping your ruler perpendicular to the top and bottom edges of the square, mark vertical lines going through the four points, exactly as shown in the diagram.

6. Turn your graph paper a one-quarter turn and repeat Step 2 through 5. This will complete the grid, exactly as shown in the diagram.

SAMPLES

Swamp Angel

There are three divisions across the top and a total of nine squares. If each division is 4″ (10 cm), the finished block measures 12″ (30 cm).

Square and Stars

There are four divisions across the top and a total of sixteen squares. If each division is 3″ (7.8 cm), the finished block measures 12″ (30 cm).

Memory

There are six divisions across the top and a total of thirty-six squares. If each division is 2″ (5 cm), the finished block measures 12″ (30 cm).

Pine Tree

There are eight divisions across the top and a total of sixty-four squares. If each division is 1½″ (4cm), the finished block measures 12″ (30 cm).

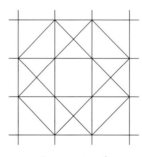

Swamp Angel

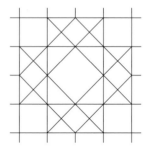

Square and Stars

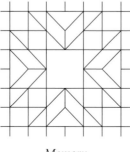

Memory

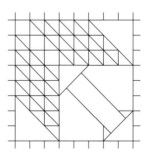

Pine Tree

PATTERN DRAFTING MADE EASY

To find out for yourself the freedom drafting your own patterns gives you, do the Practice Exercises that follow.

PRACTICE EXERCISE: Drafting *54-40 or Fight* As a 12″ (30 cm) Block

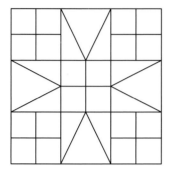

1. Using your C-Thru ruler and lead pencil, mark a 12″ (30 cm) square on the graph paper.

2. Place a dot every 4″ (10 cm) around the edge of the block. Refer to the diagram and label these points A through H.

3. Mark the following lines, making nine 4″ (10 cm) squares:

    A to F   H to C

    B to E   G to D

4. Next, mark lines in the four corner squares and the center square, dividing them in half to make four 2″ (5cm) squares in each.

5. Mark the points J, K, L, and M on the graph paper, then draw the following lines:

    A to J   C to K   E to L   G to M

    B to J   D to K   F to L   H to M

6. Place a heavy dot at points A, B, J, G, and M. These dots will be needed in the construction of the block.

There are three different template patterns in this block: #1—2″ (5 cm) squares. #2—small triangles, #3—large triangles. Mark these numbers and the direction of the lengthwise grain on the template patterns onto the graph paper.

7. Mark a ¼″ (0.75 cm) line for the seam allowance around the outside of each of the three template patterns. For accuracy, place the large C-Thru ruler over the graph paper, lining up the ¼″ (0.75 cm) mark on the ruler directly over the outline of the template pattern, so that ¼″ (0.75 cm) of the ruler extends beyond its marked line. Mark along the edge of the ruler with a red ultra-fine permanent pen.

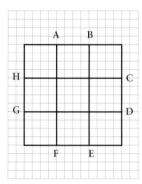

Steps 2–3

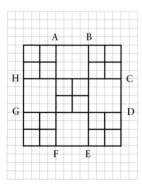

Step 4

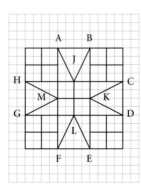

Step 5

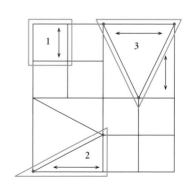

Steps 6–7

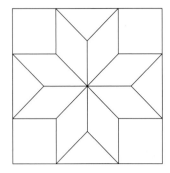

This block differs from the others because it cannot be broken down into squares. It is constructed from diagonal lines which radiate from the center. Below are instructions for drafting this star into a 12″ (30 cm) block.

1. Using the pencil, mark a 12″ (30 cm) square on the graph paper.

2. Mark diagonal lines through the square.

3. Use the ruler or compass to determine the measurement from the center point of the square to the right-hand corner.

4. Use this measurement to mark the distance from the right-hand corner to points A and D.

5. Using the same measurement, continue in the same manner with the remaining three corners to mark in points B, C, E, F, G, and H.

6. Mark the following lines:

A to D	A to F	C to F	C to H
B to G	B to E	E to H	D to G

7. Mark in points I, J, K, and L.

8. Mark lines from I to K and J to L

9. Use an eraser to eliminate the lines running through the corner squares and the diamonds.

10. There are three template patterns: #1 (squares), #2 (triangles), and #3 (diamonds). Mark these numbers and the direction of the lengthwise grain on the patterns on the graph paper.

11. Mark a ¼″ (0.75 cm) line for the seam allowance around the outside of each of the three template patterns. For accuracy, place the large C-Thru ruler over the graph paper, lining up the ¼″ (0.75 cm) mark on the ruler directly over the outline of the template pattern, so that ¼″ (0.75 cm) of the ruler extends beyond the marked line. Mark along the edge of the ruler with a red ultra-fine permanent pen.

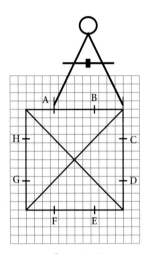

Steps 1–5

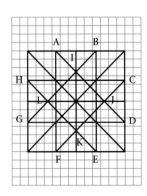

Steps 6–8

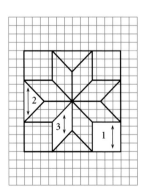

Step 10

TEMPLATES AND THEIR USES

This section contains two Practice Exercises involving templates: making templates and marking and cutting fabric using templates. The instructions given are specifically for *54-40 or Fight.* No general instructions are given for these techniques. *Warning:* We strongly recommend that all beginners work through the following Practice Exercises.

PRACTICE EXERCISE: Making Templates for *54-40 or Fight*

1. Place the drafted pattern on your cutting board. Lay a piece of template plastic over the pattern and tape it in place around the edges.

2. Some template plastic can be scored (lightly cut through the surface only) and then folded to separate. If you are able to obtain such plastic, proceed as follows. Place your wide plastic ruler on top of the template plastic with the edge of the ruler directly over one of the red cutting lines made on the drafted pattern. Use your rotary cutter to score the plastic on this line. Continue in the same manner around the other sides of this particular template pattern. Remove the template plastic from the graph paper. Fold the plastic on the scored lines to break off the individual template. Repeat for the other two template patterns.

3. If you are not able to obtain the template plastic described above, proceed as follows. With the template plastic placed over the drafted pattern, use a permanent pen and large C-Thru ruler to mark the three template patterns on the template plastic, following the red lines. Remove the graph paper from under the template plastic. Place the template plastic on the cutting board and tape it in place. Lay the edge of the wide plastic ruler directly over the marked line on the plastic. Use a rotary cutter to cut the templates apart, cutting just inside the line.

4. Lay the cut templates on top of the drafted pattern to see that they are accurate and that *the seam allowance has been added to all sides.* Also, be certain to mark the heavy dots on the triangular templates.

5. Use a permanent pen to write on each template:

> Block: *54-40 or Fight*
> Template: #1, 2, or 3
> Block size: 12″ (30 cm)
> Direction of lengthwise grain

Now that you have made the templates, move on to the next exercise on marking and cutting your fabric.

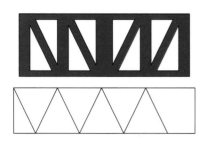

1. With the wrong side facing up, place a single thickness of fabric on top of the rough side of a piece of sandpaper. Lay the plastic template for *54-40 or Fight* on top of the fabric, making sure the lengthwise marking on the template corresponds to the lengthwise grain of the fabric. Using a pencil, mark around the template. Do not press so hard as to push the true size of the template pattern out of shape. If you are using a *nondirectional* fabric, you can cut up to four thicknesses simultaneously. Make sure the fabric has a smooth surface and the selvages are even. Keep the folds in place with either a light pressing or a few pins. If you are using a *directional* printed fabric, you will not be able to see how the layers underneath are being cut, so you will want to cut a single thickness.

Cut the following for your practice block:

Light fabric—cut ten of Template #1 and four of Template #3

Medium fabric—cut ten of Template #1

Dark fabric—cut eight of Template #2 (four right side up and four wrong side up, so they will be mirror images)

2. If you are cutting just one thickness of fabric, use sharp scissors and take long cutting strokes. If you are cutting multiple layers and using scissors, pin the fabrics together inside the outline of the template pattern to keep the layers united and prevent them from slipping.

3. Transfer the heavy dots from the templates onto the wrong sides of the triangular fabric pieces.

Chapter 12

SAMPLER QUILT

 The sampler quilt is an ideal introduction to quiltmaking. It offers the quiltmaker a wide range of basic techniques to master while constructing a variety of pieced and appliquéd quilt block patterns. Working through the many aspects of quiltmaking from fabric selection and color choices to the final binding provides the student with a solid foundation. Students learn the importance of accuracy every step of the way and gain the confidence and techniques required to make repeated block pattern quilts before progressing to some of the more complex patterns.

CLASS OUTLINE

The class outline that follows includes thirteen pieced and appliquéd quilt block patterns. It covers a wide range of basic techniques, including quick-cutting, half-square triangles, double half-square triangles, templates, curves, Y-seams, eight-point star construction, and appliqué. If you wish to substitute blocks, choosing from among the patterns in the book, you may do so.

CLASS ONE	*Nine-Patch*—ten blocks
CLASS TWO	*Log Cabin*—one 12″ (30 cm) or four 6″ (15 cm)
CLASS THREE	*Madison House*
CLASS FOUR	*Bear's Paw* and *Swamp Angel*
CLASS FIVE	*Sawtooth Star*—four blocks—and *Madison House Tree* —two blocks
CLASS SIX	*Memory* and *Squares and Stars*
CLASS SEVEN	*Drunkard's Path* and *Attic Windows*
CLASS EIGHT	*Heart* and *Kaleidoscope*—four blocks each
CLASS NINE	Settings and Borders
CLASS TEN	Layering and Basting
CLASS ELEVEN	Quilting and Binding (demonstrations)

Lawry's Sampler, Lawry Thorn, quilted by Katrina Beverage

LaVonne's Sampler, LaVonne J. Horner, quilted by Angelia Haworth

Cynthia's Sampler,
Cynthia Sherburne, quilted
by Kathy Sandbach

Diana and Laura's Sampler, quilted by Paula Reid

Katie's Sampler, Katie Prindle, quilted by Debra Dann

*Patti's Sampler,
Patti Scott-Baier, quilted
by Mary Bertken*

SAMPLER BLOCKS

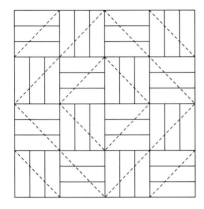

ROMAN SQUARE (*page 14*)

Makes one 12″ (30 cm) block
Twelve 1½″ × 15″ (4 cm × 38 cm) pieces (four light and eight dark)

 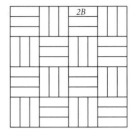

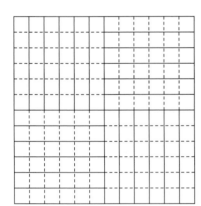

FENCE RAIL (*page 16*)

Makes one 12″ (30 cm) block
Six 1½″ (4 cm) strips, graduated in color from light to dark. See the Practice Exercise on page 102 for help

 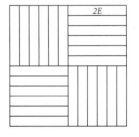

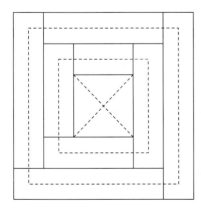

LOG CABIN (*page 18*)

Makes four 6″ (15 cm) blocks
1D: Four 2½″ (6.5 cm) squares
2A and 2B: One 1½″ (4 cm) strip (light)
2B and 2C: One 1½″ (4 cm) strip (dark)
2C and 2D: One 1½″(4 cm) strip (light)
2D and 2E: Two 1½″ (4 cm) strips (dark)

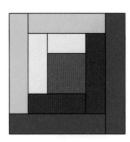 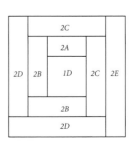

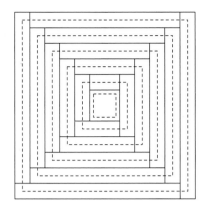

LOG CABIN (page 18)

Makes one 12″ (30 cm) block
Center: One 2½″ (6.5 cm) square
Strips: Ten 1½″ (4 cm) strips (five light, five dark). Excess is trimmed during construction

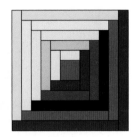
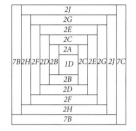

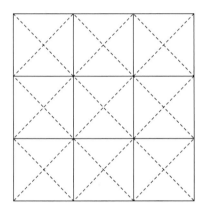

NINE-PATCH (page 22)

Makes ten 6″ (15 cm) blocks
Three 2½″ (6.5 cm) strips (each of two fabrics)

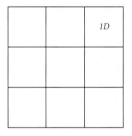

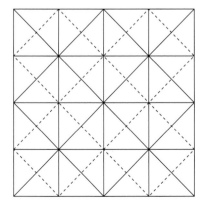

PINWHEEL (page 32)

Makes four 6″ (15 cm) blocks
Sixteen 3⅞″ (10 cm) squares, cut in half diagonally (eight light, eight dark)

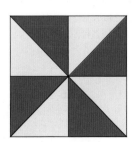
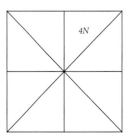

OCEAN WAVES (page 34)

Makes one 12″ (30 cm) block
4U: Twenty-four 3″ (7.9 cm) squares, cut in half diagonally (twelve light, twelve dark)
1K: One 6½″ (16.5 cm) square

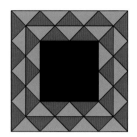 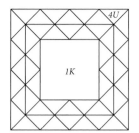

WILD GOOSE CHASE VARIATION (page 38)

Makes one 12″ (30 cm) block
1K: One 6½″ (16.5 cm) square
1F: Four 3½″ (9 cm) squares (two light, two dark)
4Q: Thirty-two 2″ (5.3 cm) squares (sixteen each of two fabrics)
4J: Sixteen 2″ × 3½″ (5.3 cm × 9 cm) pieces (eight each of two fabrics)

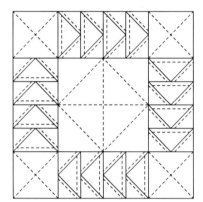

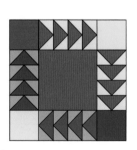 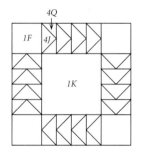

SAWTOOTH STAR (page 40)

Makes four 6″ (15 cm) blocks
Background
1C: Sixteen 2″ (5.5 cm) squares
4J: Sixteen 2″ × 3½″ (5.5 cm × 9cm) pieces
Star
4Q: Thirty-two 2″ (5.5 cm) squares
1C: Sixteen 2″ (5.5 cm) squares

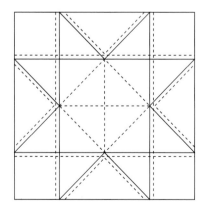

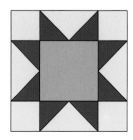 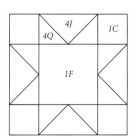

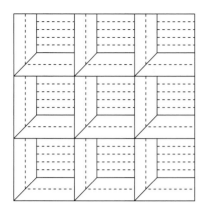

ATTIC WINDOWS (page 42)

Makes one 12″ (30 cm) block
1E: Nine 3″ (7.8 cm) squares
7D: Three 2″ (5.5 cm) strips with template
7DR*: Three 2″ (5.5 cm) strips with template
* R= *reverse template on fabric*

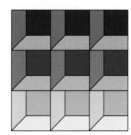
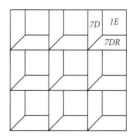

SPOOL (page 44)

Makes four 6″ (15 cm) blocks
1D: Four 2½″ (6.5 cm) squares
7A: Eight each for spools and background. These can be quick-cut with 2½″ (6.5 cm) wide strips and using the template to mark the angles

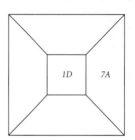

MADISON HOUSE (*page 46*)

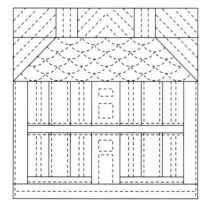

Makes one 12″ (30 cm) block

Sky
2E: Two 1½″ × 6½″ (4 cm × 16.5 cm) pieces
1L: Two 2½″ × 3½″ (6.5 cm × 9 cm) pieces
1M: One 2½″ × 4½″ (6.5 cm × 11.5 cm) piece
4N: Two 3½″ (9 cm) squares

Chimneys
2A: Two 1½″ × 2½″ (3.4 cm × 6.5 cm) pieces

Roof
6G: One 3½″ × 12½″ (9 cm × 31.5 cm) piece

House
3M: Two 1⅞″ × 13″ (4.9 cm × 34 cm) pieces

Windows

3M: One 1⅞″ × 13″ (4.9 cm × 34 cm) piece

Upper door

3H: One 2¼″ × 3″ (6.7 cm × 7.7 cm) piece

Lower door

3J: One 2¼″ × 3½″ (6.7 cm × 9 cm) piece

Upper balcony

3G: One 1″ × 10½″ (2.8 cm × 26.5 cm) piece

Lower balconies

3E: Two 1″ × 4⅝″ (2.8 cm × 11.7 cm) pieces

Ground

7C: One 1½″ × 12½″ (3.4 cm × 31.5 cm) piece

Note: Use the double half-square triangle technique to construct the sky/roof unit. See page 104 for help. See Step 2 diagram on page 49 for house/window construction.

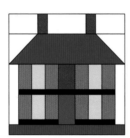
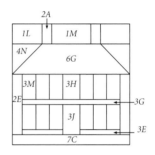

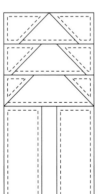

MADISON HOUSE TREE *(page 46)*

Makes two 6″ × 12″ (15 cm × 30 cm) blocks

Background

5D and 5DR*: Four 2½″ × 3½″ (6.5 cm × 9 cm) pieces

5C and 5CR*: Four 2½″ × 3″ (6.5 cm × 7.8 cm) pieces

4P: Four 2½″ (6.5 cm) squares

3L: Four 3″ × 6½″ (7.8 cm × 16.5 cm) pieces

Tree

4F: Two 2½″ × 4½″ (6.5 cm × 11.5 cm) pieces

5F: Two 2½″ × 5½″ (6.5 cm × 14 cm) pieces

5E: Two 2½″ × 6½″ (6.5 cm × 16.5 cm) pieces

2E: Two 1½″ × 6½″ (4 cm × 16.5 cm) pieces

* *R=reverse template on fabric*

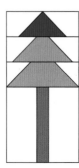
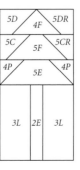

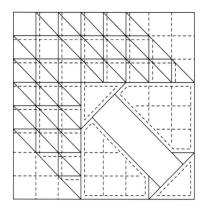

PINE TREE (page 50)

Makes one 12″ (30 cm) block

Background

1C: Three 2″ (5.3 cm) squares, cut in half diagonally
4Q: Twelve 2⅜″ (6.3 cm) squares, cut in half diagonally
4N: One 3⅞″ (10 cm) square, cut in half diagonally (use one triangle)
4L: One 5⅜″ (13.8 cm) square, cut in half diagonally
5B and 5BR*: One 6⅞″ (17.5 cm) square, cut in half diagonally. Use Template 5B to cut angles (one and one reversed)
*R=reverse template on fabric

Tree

4Q: Fifteen 2⅜″ (6.3 cm) squares, cut in half diagonally
4R: One 1⅞″ (5 cm) square, cut in half diagonally
4N: One 3⅞″ (10 cm) square, cut in half diagonally (use one triangle)
8E: One 2⅝″ × 6⅞″ (6.9 × 17.7 cm) piece

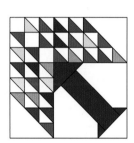 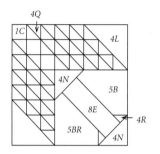

BEAR'S PAW (page 53)

Makes one 12″(30 cm) block

Background

2P: Four 2⅛″ (5.5 cm) squares
4A: Eight 2½″ (6.5 cm) squares, cut in half diagonally
3N: Four 2¾″ × 5⅜″ (7.5 cm × 13.5 cm) pieces

Design

2T: Four 3¾″ (9.5 cm) squares
2Q: One 2¾″ (7.5 cm) square
4A: Eight 2½″(6.5 cm) squares, cut in half diagonally

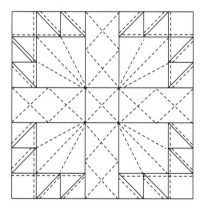

 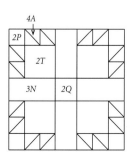

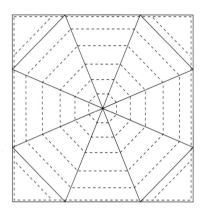

KALEIDOSCOPE *(page 56)*

Makes four 6″ (15 cm) blocks
4B: Eight 2⅝″ (6.7 cm) squares, cut in half diagonally
5A: Thirty-two pieces
—OR—
Cut 4″ (10 cm) wide strips and use template to mark the angles

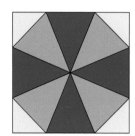
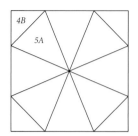

HEART *(page 60)*

Makes four 6″ (15 cm) blocks
1K: Four 6½″ (16.5 cm) squares
4S: Four with template.

POSTAGE STAMP BASKETS *(page 62)*

Makes four 6″ (15 cm) blocks

Background
4M: Four 4⅞″ (12.5 cm) squares, cut in half diagonally
1D: Eight 2½″ (6.5 cm) squares

Basket
4P: Four 2⅞″ (7.5 cm) squares, cut in half diagonally
4M: Four 4⅞″ (12.5 cm) squares, cut in half diagonally
8D: Use the remaining four (4M) triangles with Template 8D for handles

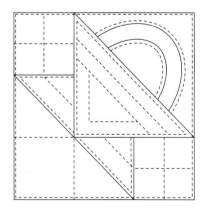

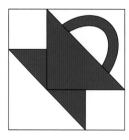
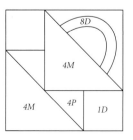

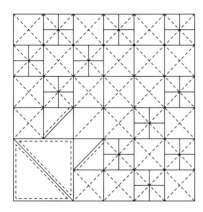

BLOSSOMING TREE (page 72)

Makes one 12" (30 cm) block

Background

1D: One 2½" (6.5 cm) strip, cut into sixteen 2½" (6.5 cm) squares

4P: One 2⅞" (7.5 cm) square, cut in half diagonally

4M: One 4⅞" (12.5 cm) square, cut in half diagonally (use one triangle)

Tree

1B: Eight 1½" × 14" (4 cm × 35 cm) pieces (four light and four dark)

1D: Three 2½" (6.5 cm) squares

4P: One 2⅞" (7.5 cm) square, cut in half diagonally

4M: One 4⅞" (12.5 cm) square, cut in half diagonally (use one triangle)

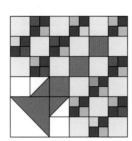

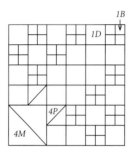

DRUNKARD'S PATH (page 75)

Makes one 12" (30 cm) block

3Q: Eight 3½" (9 cm) squares each of two fabrics. Then use the template to mark the curve

3R: Eight 2½" (7.8 cm) squares each of two fabrics. Then the template to mark the curve

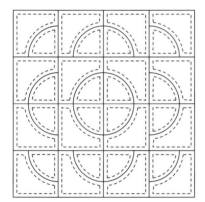

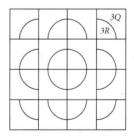

MEMORY (page 84)

Makes one 12″ (30 cm) block

4P: Eight 2⅞″ (7.5 cm) squares, four each of two fabrics cut in half diagonally
    Sixteen 2½″ (6.5 cm) squares, eight each of two fabrics
4F: Eight 2½″ × 4½″ (6.5 cm × 11.5 cm) pieces, four each of two fabrics
1D: Eight 2½″ (6.5 cm) squares
1H: One 4½″ (11.5 cm) square

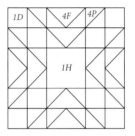

54-40 OR FIGHT (page 84)

Makes one 12″ (30 cm) block
1D: Twenty 2½″ (6.5 cm) squares
8A and 8AR*: Four and four reversed with template
8B: Four with template
*R=reverse template on fabric

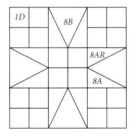

SWAMP ANGEL (page 84)

Makes one 12″ (30 cm) block
4M: Four 4⅞″ (12.5 cm) squares, cut in half diagonally (two each of two fabrics)
1H: One 4½″ (11.5 cm) square
4F: Four 5¼″ (13.6 cm) squares, cut in quarters diagonally (two each of two fabrics)

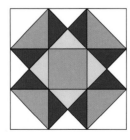
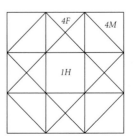

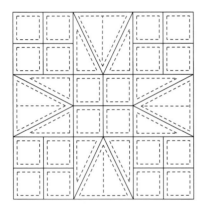

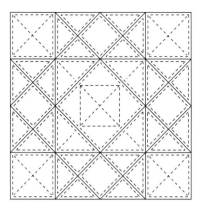

SQUARE AND STARS *(page 85)*

Makes one 12″ (30 cm) block

2S: Four 2⅝″ (6.8 cm) squares
2U: One 4¾″ (12.1 cm) square
4N: Two 3⅞″ (10 cm) squares, cut in half diagonally
4J: Six 4¼″ (11.1 cm) squares, cut into quarters diagonally
1F: Four 3½″ (9 cm) squares

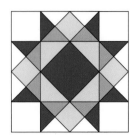
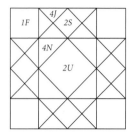

VARIABLE STAR *(page 85)*

Makes one 12″ (30 cm) block

1H: Five 4½″ (11.5 cm) squares
4F: Four 5¼″ (13.6 cm) squares (one for background, two for star points, and one for inner triangles). Then cut each square into quarters diagonally

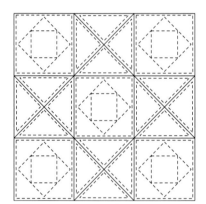
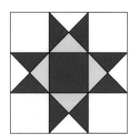
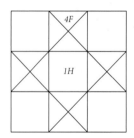

LE MOYNE STAR *(page 85)*

Makes one 12″ (30 cm) block

1G: Four 4″ (10.3 cm) squares
4E: One 6¼″ (16.1 cm) square, cut in quarters diagonally
6D: Eight with template

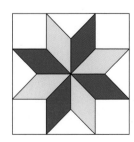
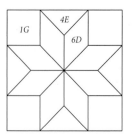

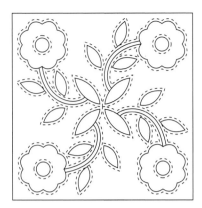

BENICIA ROSE *(page 111)*

Makes one 12″ (30 cm) block

Background
One 12½″ (31.5 cm) square

Flower
Center: Four with template
Blossom: Four with template
Leaves: Four large and twelve small with templates
Stem: 20″ (50 cm) of ¼″ (0.75 cm) finished bias.

Note: See templates on page 168 and Practice Exercise on page 111

TEMPLATES

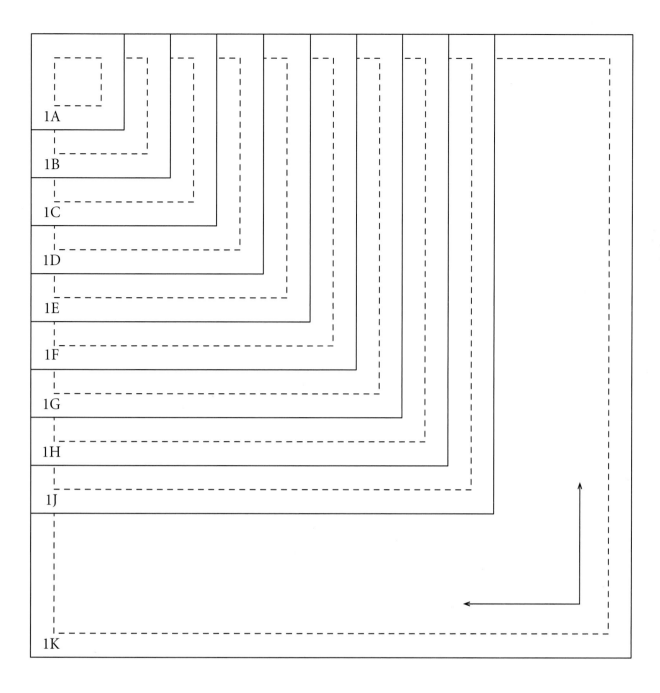

1A

1B

1C

1D

1E

1F

1G

1H

1J

1K

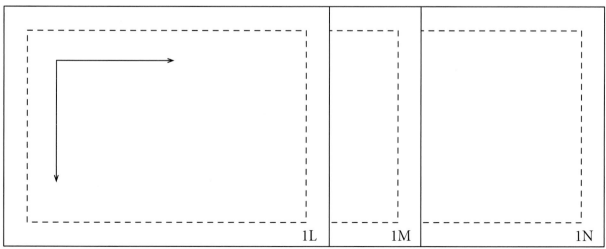

1L

1M

1N

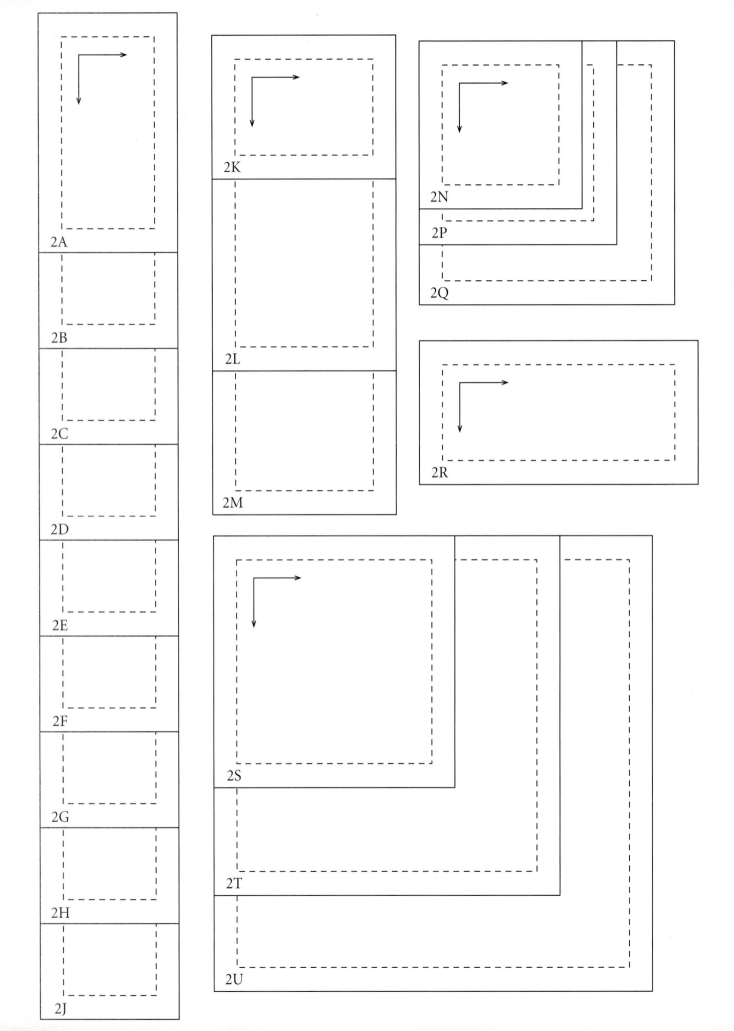

2A

2B

2C

2D

2E

2F

2G

2H

2J

2K

2L

2M

2N

2P

2Q

2R

2S

2T

2U

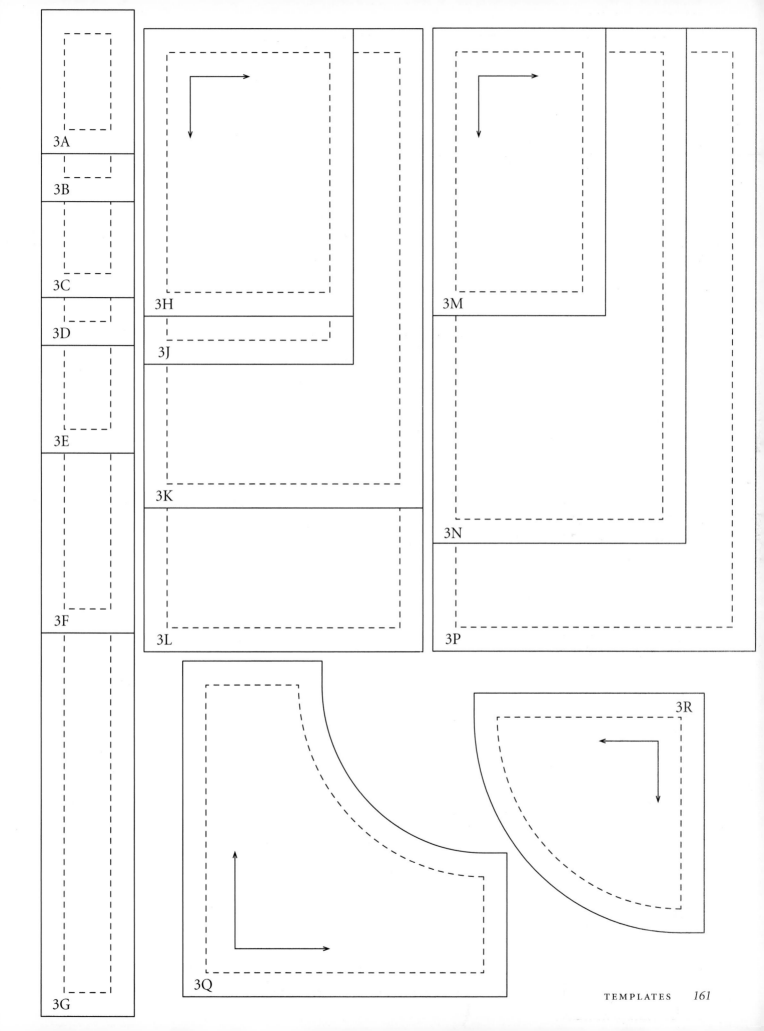

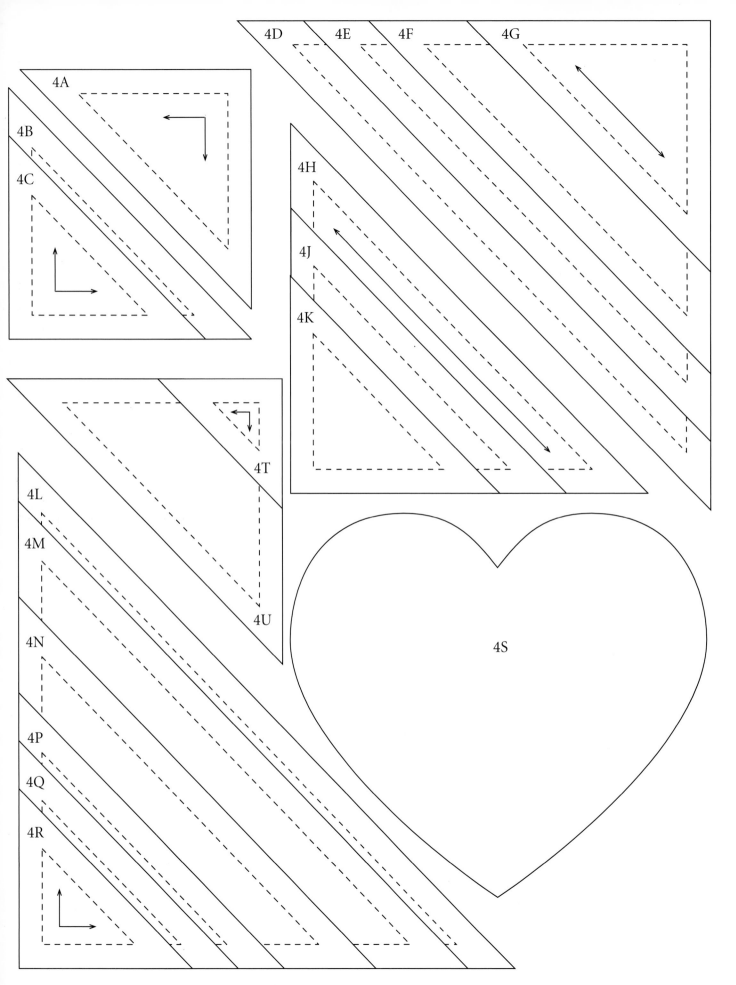

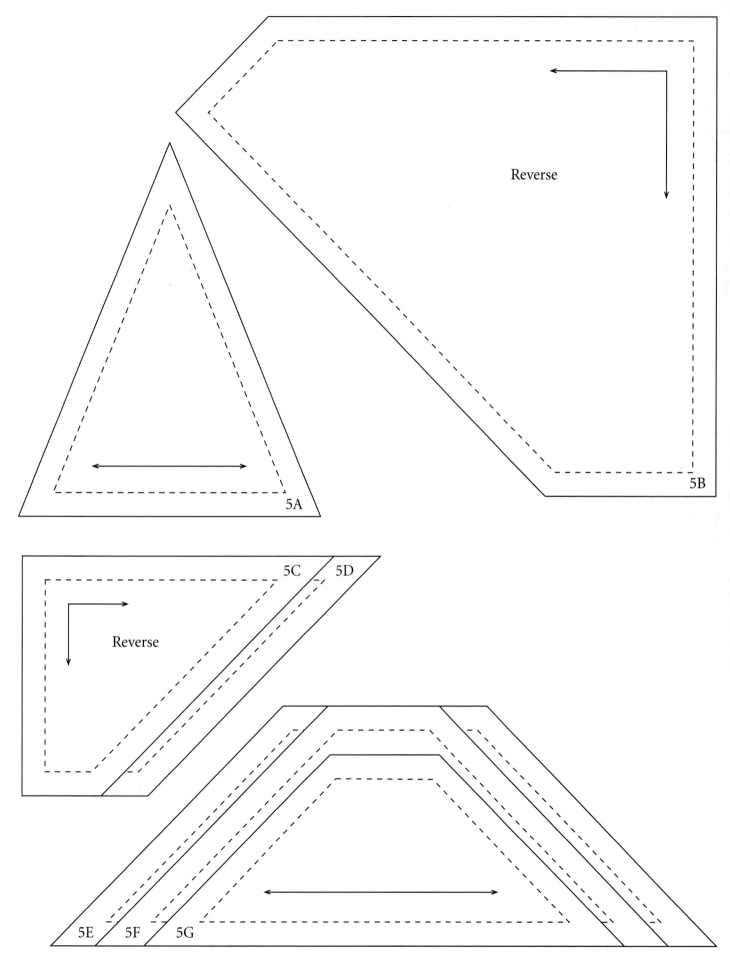

Reverse

5A

5B

5C 5D

Reverse

5E 5F 5G

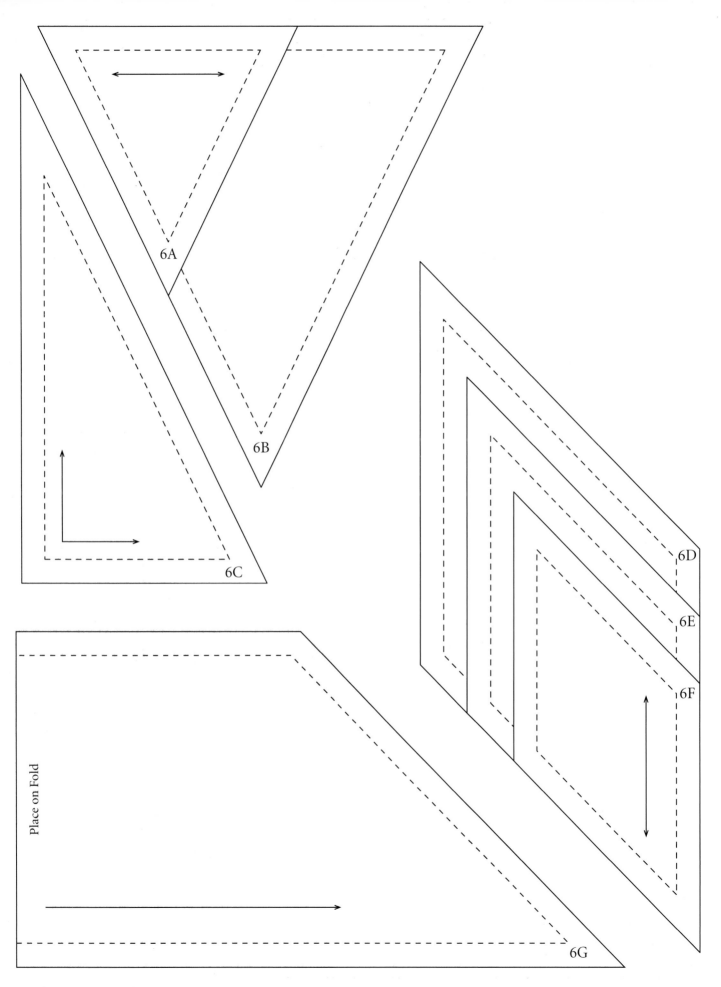

6A

6B

6C

6D

6E

6F

Place on Fold

6G

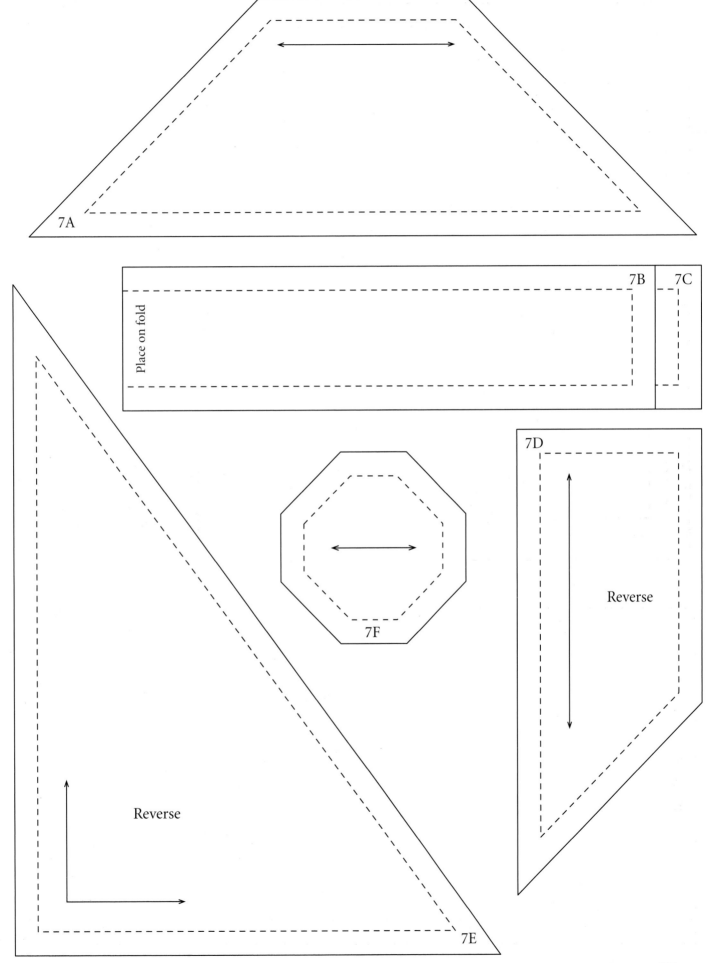

7A

7B

7C

Place on fold

7D

Reverse

7F

Reverse

7E

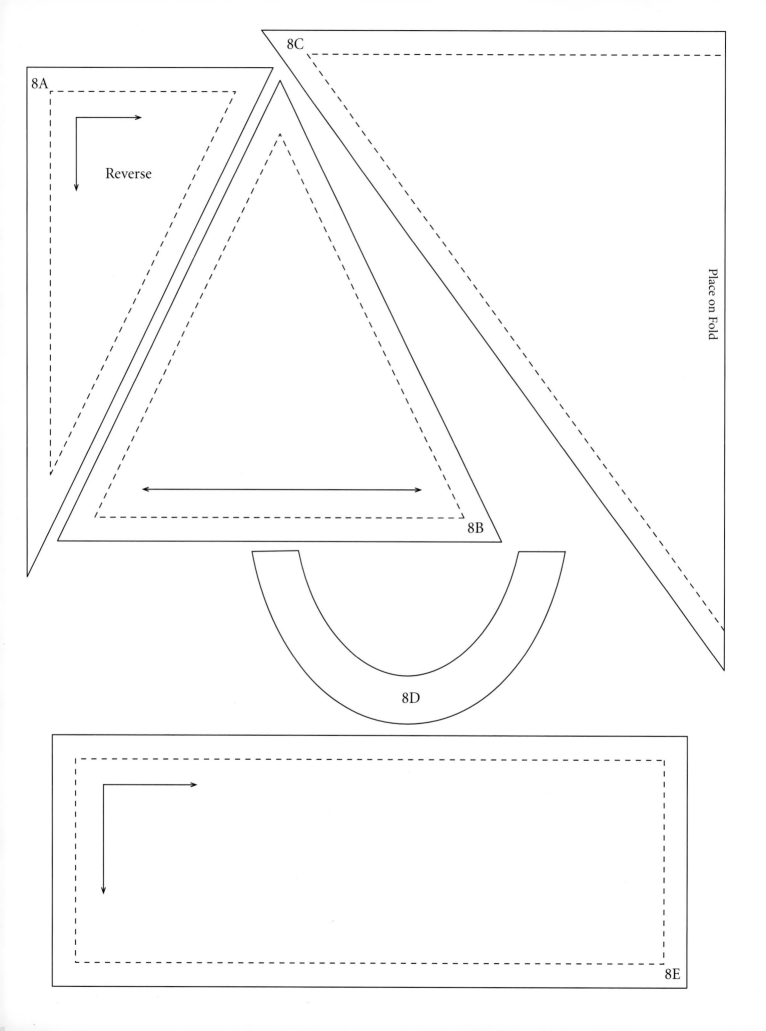

8C

8A

Reverse

Place on Fold

8B

8D

8E

One fourth of *Benicia Rose* block

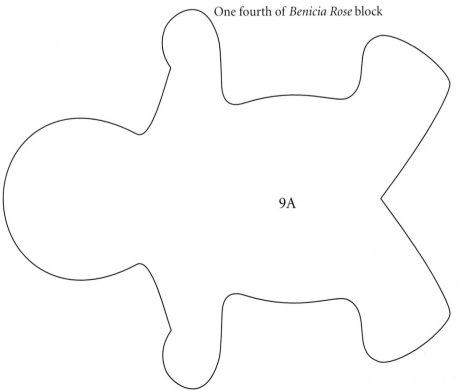

9A

GLOSSARY

Alternate block set. Pieced blocks that are combined or alternated with plain blocks.

Appliqué. A design made by cutting shapes of one or more fabrics and applying them to the surface of another.

Backing. The fabric which forms the bottom layer of the quilt.

Backstitch. These are very short stitches used at the beginning or end of a line of stitching to secure threads. These are used instead of knots. Leave a 1″/2.5 cm tail of thread at each end of the stitching line. Use a single strand of thread.

Back whipstitch. For hand appliqué work, use a single strand of thread and secure one end with a knot. With the right side of the design facing up, bring the needle and thread up from the underside out through the folded edge in the design. Insert the tip of the needle directly behind and a little below the point where the thread emerges. Without pulling the thread through, slant the needle and bring it to the top side through the folded edge in the design, approximately 1⁄16″ (0.2 cm) away from the previous stitch. Pull the thread through.

Baste. A means of loosely securing layers together temporarily.

Basting stitch. Temporary stitches used to hold fabric in place. Use a single strand of thread.

    Running basting stitch. Use the same technique as described in running stitch, but with a longer stitch.

    Diagonal basting stitch. Long, parallel diagonal stitches on the right side of the quilt, joined on the wrong side by horizontal stitches.

Batting. The filling that goes between the quilt top and the backing. It provides thickness and warmth to the quilt.

Bias. The diagonal of a woven fabric in which a true 45° angle is formed. The bias has the greatest amount of stretch.

Binding. A narrow strip of fabric used to enclose the raw edges of the quilt top, batting and backing. It can be cut on the straight grain or on the bias.

Block. See Pattern. Most of the patterns in this book are made up into 6″ (15 cm) or 12″ (30 cm) blocks.

Border. Plain, pieced or appliquéd band(s) of fabric surrounding the central section of the quilt top.

Chain/chaining. A term used to describe the method of connecting sewn pairs of pattern pieces, one behind the other, in the sewing machine, without breaking the thread connecting them.

Directional fabric. Fabric having a directional print (either horizontal, vertical, or diagonal).

Drafted pattern. Outline of the individual parts of a pattern block, made on graph paper.

Grain. The lengthwise and crosswise threads of a woven fabric. The lengthwise threads (or lengthwise grain) run parallel to the selvage edges of the fabric. This has the least amount of stretch. The crosswise threads (or crosswise grain) run perpendicular to the selvage edges and have a little more stretch than the lengthwise grain.

Grainline. The lengthwise or crosswise grain of the fabric.

Grid. Squares of uniform size.

Ground fabric. A fabric or fabrics used as the background in a pattern block.

Hand quilting. Small running stitches which hold the three layers of the quilt together, either following a design which has been marked on the quilt top or following the outline of a pieced or appliquéd block.

Layering. The process of placing the three layers of the quilt together.

Loft. The springiness, or fluffiness, of a fiber.

Machine quilting. Machine stitches which hold the three layers of the quilt together.

Miter. Vertical and horizontal strips of fabric are joined at 45° angles, forming a 90° corner. Mitered corners can be used in constructing borders.

Non-directional fabric. A printed fabric without a direction, such as an all-over print.

Pattern. Any design of a quilt usually repeated several times on the quilt top. Sometimes referred to as "design."

Perle cotton. A two-ply cotton yarn with a high twist and a silk-like finish.

Piecing/pieced block. Pieces of cut fabric sewn together to produce a pattern, usually in the form of a block.

Posts. Squares of fabric joining sashing to sashing.

Quilt top. The top layer of the quilt. It can be pieced, appliquéd or a combination of the two.

Quilting/quilting stitches. Stitches used to secure the three layers of the quilt together. The quilting can be done by either hand or machine.

Running stitch. A short, even stitch used for hand piecing.

Sashing. The strip of fabric used between blocks to separate and set them together.

Seam. The stitched junction of two pieces of fabric, right sides together, with a ¼" (0.75 cm) allowance. Can be done by either hand or machine.

Seam allowance. The distance between the cut edge of the fabrics and the stitching line. In quiltmaking this is ¼" (0.75 cm).

Selvage. The finished edges of a woven fabric on the lengthwise threads.

Set/setting. The arrangement in which individual blocks are sewn together. A diagonal or straight setting is commonly used.

Sew order. The sequence of sewing individual pieces or units together to form a block.

Slip stitch. This is a small, almost invisible, stitch used to secure a folded edge to a flat surface. Use a single strand of thread and secure one end with a knot. To secure a binding, bring the needle directly behind where the thread emerged, catching only a few threads of the backing fabric. Without pulling the thread through, bring the needle up through the fold in the binding approximately ⅛" (0.5 cm) away from the previous stitch.

Square knot. Bring the left thread over and around the right thread. Then, cross the right thread in front of the left and bring it through the loop. Pull both ends to tighten the knot.

Template. An individual model of a part of a pattern block made from template plastic.

Tying. A quick method of securing the three layers of the quilt together.

INDEX

ABOUT THE AUTHORS

Diana McClun's career as a quiltmaker blossomed in mid-life, but was inspired much earlier. As a toddler in her mothers kitchen Diana recalls hours spent playing with fabric scraps wisely kept in the flour drawer while her mother worked. College found Diana at the University of Idaho, studying cothing and textiles. Her passion for fiber grew during the years she was raising a family. In 1970, Diana enrolled at San Jose State University to study fine arts. Eventually her love of fabric led her to San Francisco State University and further study of textiles. By 1980, Diana was ready to pursue a dream in working in the creative art of quilt-making. With her training in education, art, and textiles, she opened a business called Empty Spools in Alamo, California, centered around fabric and quiltmaking

It was during this time that college graduate Laura Nownes was seeking a new career using her artistic gifts. As a child, Laura loved to sew and her mother encouraged her fascination with fabric. Every school sewing class was a step toward understanding the joys and complexities of quiltmaking. Laura became a quiltmaking instructor and store manager at Empty Spools.

Diana and Laura began a friendship that led to the creation of *Quilts! Quilts!! Quilts!!!,* the book that has inspired literally hundreds of thousands of new quilters to take up this traditional American art form. They have worked together on television programs, with study groups, and in seminars, through which they continue to inspire in others a life-long love of quiltmaking. Diana and Laura have written three other successful books on quiltmaking.

Quilts! Quilts!! Quilts!!! Instructor's Guide

The **Quilts! Quilts!! Quilts!!! Instructor's Guide** is filled with important information that will help quilting teachers plan, prepare for, and conduct classes. It includes lesson plans, guidance on teaching basic quilting skills, alternative choices for planning a sampler class, machine-quilting designs, and other teaching resources. Ask your local bookstore or fabric store or contact the publisher. (ISBN: 0-8442-2618-1)